THE FIRST YEAR

OF MY DEATH

THE FIRST YEAR
OF MY DEATH

Mary Stein

POPPING LEAF BOOKS

Cover photo courtesy of Richard Whittaker

ISBN 978-0-9979083-2-9

For all my teachers

CHAPTER 1: "OUT OF THERE!"

ALMOST EMBRACING, our bodies lay together in the wreckage of our car. My ebbing blood poured over Claire and mingled with the pooling blood of her shattered hand.

Sirens crescendoed and fell silent. Jammed metal cried out, a door was wrenched open, hands reached in. Our bodies were parted and lifted into an ambulance, mine up front near the driver, Claire's in the back, where a paramedic in green scrubs worked over her.

They brought in a young man, bleeding heavily, and placed his stretcher next to Claire's, the two stretchers touching. As they inserted an IV in his arm, the attendants exchanged comments.

"With damage to the cars like that, he must have been going 50."

"Or 60, and through an intersection. . . on a red light,

apparently."

"How's she doing?"

"She's lost a lot of blood. Her hand is smashed."

"Can she live?"

"Probably. But he's gone."

"Her hand is drenched with his blood. It's like he was trying to give her a transfusion."

The ambulance screamed and bumped its way down the tarred-over patchwork of Mission Street in San Francisco. A big jolt popped out the young man's IV, and one of his wounds arced a stream of blood on Claire's hand.

"*Awwrrkk.*" I made out a shadowy form beside Claire. "Did you see that? The blood of the driver who rammed them, entering her blood stream?"

Another shadow spoke. "Yes, and now the three of them are reconciled in her living blood! Wonderful! It's an intended event."

A third, deeper voice drawled, "Not wonderful quite yet, Mallard."

"Reconciled? *Awwrrkk.* Her blood, her husband's blood, and the blood of his killer, mixing in her body? The woman's a battlefield." The first shadow motioned toward where I hovered over the scene. "And now he's here, yanked out of where he was perfectly comfortable. There'll be trouble."

The eager voice said, "Well, he's not stuck now, and I'm glad. It was a Request, don't forget."

"Mistakes get made. What are his chances of getting up to speed? *Quawwkkk.*"

8

Then I remembered — the scream of metal, the pressure, the shatter of glass, the shards of pain that burst me open like a knifed drum. The swift descent toward heavy warm darkness. Where I'd sleep . . . and sleep some more . . .

But a keen cry had pierced the darkness:

OUT OF THERE! OUT!

I burst from the comforting gloom of my body, with hanks of heavy stuff, like sea muck or rotting weeds, trailing after me. And now my spent body lay below me as the ambulance rocked into the driveway of St. James's Hospital in San Francisco.

CHAPTER 2: THE ANIMALS

AT THE HOSPITAL Claire was hurried into the ER, while my body rolled off in another direction. A longing seized me to be back inside the familiar tent of flesh, and I caught a ride on the handle of the gurney as it sped down the hall and through double doors marked "morgue."

I was in the quiet room I'd seen so often in police procedurals: the bare white walls, the laboratory sink, the adjustable-height post-mortem platforms, the walk-in refrigerator doors. A white-suited young man motioned the paramedic who was pushing the gurney toward a side of the room lighted by high windows above and a spotlight on the wall below them that shone down on my shrouded body. The paramedic signed a paper and left, and the young man in the white outfit went back to his desk.

Beneath me the dangling shreds trembled with excitement, like kids in a candy shop, urging me to return home to my body. At the same time, I felt a feather-light pull, as an extraordinarily fine thread emerged from my navel, stretched across the room and passed through the double doors of the morgue. As I approached my body, the pull of the Thread weakened, like a shy animal in retreat, while the tatters stepped up their clamor. *Here. Fall. Rest. Stay. Here. Fall. Rest.*

I reached out toward what lay beneath the sheet, to the promise of rest, of welcome surrender. I'd slip into my body, let it cradle me. *Sleep . . .*

"Oh, my dear, my dear." In a rush of wings, a large brown-and-beige bird alighted and stood between me and my sheet-draped body. I recognized one of the shadowy silhouettes from the ambulance. A shapely mallard, five feet tall, with the intricate brown dappling and wise look of female mallards, put out a cautionary wing. "You mustn't lose connection. What would she do?" The Mallard's quacks were close to sobs.

The tatters stepped up their tattoo. *Here. Fall, Rest. Stay. Now. Here. Fall.*

"Connection--to Claire?"

"To Claire! Yes, yes! You must follow the Thread. If you stay here," She looked toward the body on the gurney, "it will be such a loss." The Mallard's eyes glistened.

Loss? Claire?

The return to my stiffening body horrified me.

11

I flew back toward the door I'd come through and pulled desperately at its handle. Surely it had opened inward. I grabbed at the handle, my substance shaking and pulling and pushing again at the door, at which it opened abruptly and I was in the hallway, speeding toward the emergency room.

Claire, I'm here, I whispered. A nurse, one hand on Claire's shoulder, was checking electronic reports of her condition as she lay unconscious among the harsh lights. Above the throbbing life-support machines, a high humming sounded. Claire might have joked that it was the sound of the doctors and nurses and interns praying for her as they gave her a transfusion. I would have questioned that. How many doctors did she think spent time praying in the emergency zone--or praying at all? And what did she mean by prayer? But arguing with me had never interested her, and I had to wait for a session of the Skeptics Society to bring up such questions with the journalists like myself, the scientists, and the assorted iconoclasts who came to the Skeptics' meetings.

Amid the mindless drone of the machines, I pictured a presentation to the Society in which I questioned whether consciousness needed a body. I'd mention the thundering demand that released me from my own body and the shadowy voices I'd heard in the ambulance. But I hesitated to speak about the tatters or the strange warning that drew me back to the ER. As an investigator of psychic claims, I had dismissed for lack of evidence reports claiming to come from the Other

Side. And now I'd be delivering one of those pathetic reports.

They moved her into the operating room, and I watched, while a tall gray-haired man, his eyes compassionate above a surgical mask, removed Claire's crushed right hand and sutured what remained of her arm. She was taken to a regular hospital room, and I stayed beside her as the night deepened and the place grew quiet. My grief took massive hold then, an ache and bite of mourning for the life we'd had, now shattered by the disregard of some reckless fool.

In her sleep, Claire tossed and murmured, cried out, returned to stillness. At each movement of her body, I felt the pluck of the Thread. The tatters subsided to dejected thumps.

When she woke up, Dr. Hurd, tallish and graying, with a quietly sympathetic look, introduced himself. He said they'd saved her arm below the elbow, almost to the wrist. "Most of your arm is still there, which is good news for rehab." She didn't hear much of what he said about a prosthesis, about the SUV broadsiding us, the "no chance for your husband," the "instantly."

Claire slept again, woke in pain. They gave her more morphine and she slept again, the rawness of the amputation throbbing through the haze of the drug.

I stayed beside her, checking out the substance I have now. I saw a familiar shape, a semi-transparent body still wearing the blue shirt and tweed jacket I had put on that morning. I liked that jacket and was glad it looked

13

fresh again. Ragged shreds, smelling like over-ripe seaweed, still dangled off my legs and feet, though the nurse who stepped on one of them didn't notice. But I had eyes that could see and a body that bore no trace of the accident.

Our daughter Judy and her husband Greg came and stood, shocked and quiet, by Claire's bed. I put my arm around Judy, whose eyes were red from crying, and laid a comforting hand on Greg's shoulder: *I'm here. I'm with you. Sorry for all this.* But they gave no indication of hearing me, and I felt isolated in my sorrow — for Claire and for myself, Claire's husband and Judy's father.

And I was angry, for the driver responsible for my death was alive and being cared for in this very hospital.

As the Lathrops left for the morgue to identify my body, the urge returned to rejoin the flesh I'd lived in comfortably for fifty-two years (though there'd been a problem lately), and the tatters began an excited clamoring. *Come . . . rest . . . sleep. . .*

Snap! In a brisk flutter of wings, Mallard's brown-and-beige body furled into place beside me, and her orange-pink webs gripped at the bedrail, her wise eyes remonstrating. "Time for the meeting. Come along, dear. *Now.*"

Her beak grasped me and lifted me by the nape of my substance the way a cat lifts her young. I twisted my head upward and saw Mallard's head slip part way into the ceiling, then stop as if she'd bumped into a barrier. Her head came back into the room, her beak still grasping me kitten-wise. She flapped onto the arm of the

14

bed table, and released me. "I see you're not fully portable, dear. Never mind, we'll make do."

Back I went into her grasp, and we flew out the door and down the hall past the nurses' station, past locked windows that Mallard deprecated in muffled tones. Finally, she spotted an air-conditioning duct and squeezed us through it, my substance slimming to a mouse's thickness as we made our way through the dark curving duct out to the roof of the hospital. I regained shape as we flew into the windy night, which brightened till it was day and we were in McLaren Park, the second largest park in San Francisco, which lies up the hill from the house where Claire and I lived. This was McLaren Park tidied up, as if the park department had come into real money and gardeners had groomed the lawns and filled the empty tiers of the planter near where we used to sit with chrysanthemums and cyclamens and snapdragons. Birds zipped here and there, coots and mallards made watery chevrons in the nearby pond, dogs lit out after sticks and balls.

Mallard deposited me on the bench of a concrete picnic table beneath an umbrella pine beside the pond. Two other creatures were already there: a formidably large raven with a slightly uneven set of beak and wised-up eyes, and a huge, serious-looking dog with a Doberman's long nose. The Dog reminded me of pictures I'd seen of Anubis, the Egyptian weigher of souls, and I was glad the more sociable mallard had brought me.

There at the picnic table I felt like a small person in a

15

tomb painting making his first nervous appearance in the afterworld. Still, I told myself that the feeling might be premature, applying to people who had definitely Passed Over. As far as I could tell I hadn't done that. I was out of my body and non-returnable, but still in San Francisco. *Forget the Egyptian stuff. Stick to the observing you've always done.* I took in the clear oval eye of Dog, Raven's hooded glance, Mallard's sturdy motherliness.

Dog spoke first in a dignified baritone. He said they were glad I had safely "arrived," and they would be providing "practical assistance" as I started my "new adventure in unusual circumstances."

"Unusual? *Quarrkkwwk.*" Raven shook his feathers impatiently. "Let's get to the point, shall we? In the accident, a few drops of your blood mixed with your wife's. Traces of you are still alive inside her. You're *connected.*" He pointed toward the slender elastic thread reaching in Claire's direction.

"I've figured that out."

"It's a dangerous situation. He doesn't get *that,* of course," he said to the others. "At least he didn't have to be yanked out this time."

"You can still be together. That's the good part. You can still be married!" Mallard gave a satisfied quack. "You *were* faithful to her, weren't you?"

My answer was going to be yes. I hadn't slept with other women after our marriage. I hadn't wanted to.

"Faithfulness? How could it mean anything to him yet? *Quaarrkkkk.*"

Mallard persisted. "But you loved her, didn't you?"

Dog looked stern, his next words close to a growl. "Too soon for that question, Mallard."

Dog's remark irritated me, but I wasn't going to make any claims he might dismiss. "Claire and I were close," I said. "I want to be near her."

Claire and I knew each other's good points and limitations, and were mostly content with each other and our long marriage. My investigations often took priority, and she accepted that.

"You can start with that wish," Dog said. He looked at the nearly invisible filament linking me and Claire. "Stay with your wife and study what is needed. Your connection with her can be strengthened. Or not."

"And it's a connection that's good for a whole year!" Mallard said. "Until the sun rises again in the same place on the horizon."

"*Quaaarrrkkk.* Responsibility without preparation. Trouble."

"And isn't responsibility what we all long to be given?" Mallard asked. "The appropriate responsibility. The hard thing that's meant just for me? *Quicquakk.*"

What was needed? I pondered Dog's remark. I've seen how a nudge in one direction or another sends people careening off, insisting on their special "needs." I've watched psychics and their clients as they follow their delusions, letting their dreams mimic, deface, and erase reality. I've seen clients fall into quagmires of belief which also sucked off significant cash.

"There's a pulse I feel," I said. "She's in pain."

Dog said, "That can guide you."

17

"There's something else," Raven said. "We weren't going to leave it out, were we?" He glanced at the others.

"Let's have it," I said.

"In the ambulance, a few drops of blood from Rick Mendoza, the driver of the SUV, fell into your wife's open wound, just as your blood did. Rich, isn't it? Your blood and his — mingled in your wife's bloodstream."

I recalled the exchange I'd overheard in the ambulance. "What kind of bastard . . . out of his mind . . . drunk . . drugged?"

Dog ignored my fury. "A good question. You're a journalist? An investigator?"

"I'm her *husband*."

"Either way. Investigate. Get the facts."

"Him? Investigate? He's already made up his mind. *Squawwkk*." I struggled to hide my irritation at the sarcastic Raven, at the super-calm Dog, and even the saccharine Mallard.

Mallard was about to speak, but at a quieting look from Dog she whispered, "No answers yet. Lovely, lovely," and beamed a bright eye at me. There followed Raven's equivalent of a Bronx cheer, and they did a fadeout.

Night had returned, the park grown silent, the trees standing under a million more stars than you ever see in the city--what you'd see in Yosemite, or out at the Nevada border. I let the dazzle pour down on me, felt calmer, and drifted along the filament back to the hospital.

18

When the brick wall turned me aside, I slipped in through the front door just as someone with a broom and dustpan came out. I wandered the halls, following the Thread until I came to where Claire slept and watched from a perch on the bedrail, the filament humming between us. Pain jolted through the thread, she cried out in her sleep, and a nurse came to adjust the sling holding her bandaged arm in place.

A small notebook appeared, open to its first creamy-gold blank page, its deep blue cover decorated with golden dragonflies. My favorite brand of ballpoint floated nearby.

I could keep a journal. And there are articles for *Scrutiny*, the periodical of the Skeptics, waiting to be completed.

I've spent years exposing mediums with their fraudulent claims of communicating with the other side. Now I'd give anything to be in touch with Claire, from wherever I am now. It's ironic, I know.

Chapter 3: Questions

I'VE SPENT the day beside Claire's bed here at St. James's, writing in this notebook. I'm trying to get clear about the tatters, which remind me of my body, not in a pleasant way. I'm not dripping eyelids and tossed-off toes, but these smelly remnants certainly hint of physical decay. When Mallard checked in, I asked her about them.

"I realize they came with the Yanking. Do I have to keep them?"

"Oh, my dear, we were so concerned about you. I kept telling Raven to take it easy, but a predator's instincts do come in. I would have preferred a gentler approach, so that we gathered all of you without the extra material." She eyed the tatters.

"*Quarrrrkkwwwkkk.*" Raven appeared. "Gentler, and we wouldn't have gotten him out. Sudden deaths are the worst. Sometimes they never figure out what happened. But in this case--" Raven paused dramatically. "With so many connections involved, and the need for speed, you're lucky. It was a quick, decisive grab."

"But do I need to keep the tatters?"

"You never know when something might come in handy, dear." Mallard reversed her head and preened her shoulder feathers.

Claire is awake today, and in pain. Mid-morning, a policeman came to take her statement and go over the details of the accident. The SUV had been witnessed as it ran a red light and crashed into the passenger side of our car, where I'd been sitting while Claire drove me to a medical appointment. Rick Mendoza, the driver, had been discharged from the army a few weeks before, after serving two years in Afghanistan. He will be charged with vehicular manslaughter--using a car as a deadly weapon. Mendoza himself is in the hospital with an assortment of serious injuries.

"I want to see John," Claire told Dr. Hurd. Her voice reached out and touched me. Speaking my name.

Dr. Hurd said, "I wouldn't advise that, Mrs. Court. Your daughter has taken care of the identification."

"But I want to be with him."

I'm here, Claire. I'm not with my body now. I stroked her

hair, my transparent fingers caressing the reddish gray-flecked auburn curls.

"What memory do you want of your husband?" It was a blunt question, though Dr. Hurd's eyes were kind.

Claire started to cry. Our closeness vanished, and the space between us felt like the distance between some imploded star and a planet green with life. I longed to be back in the car, telling her to stop at the Safeway just before the traffic light at the top of the hill. Changing everything that way.

Dog's nose sniffed out my mood, reminding me that I wasn't frozen in rigor mortis. I was in the same room with Claire. But it didn't help.

I pondered my so-called guides: Raven, with his trickster's gaze and rude comments; Mallard, the Pollyanna of ducks; Dog, whose ancestors were wolves and foxes. Who are these animal characters so brimming with authority? A duck, an outsize crow, a dog--are these to be my totem animals and guides, these run-of-the-mill creatures I knew from walks in a city park? Why not some powerful Bear or Eagle? Even an angel of modest rank?

And what about Rick Mendoza? What am I supposed to do about my unforgivably reckless killer?

A heaviness inside me passed into the Thread, and I heard the quack-click of Mallard's concern.

CHAPTER 4: SUITABLE ARRANGEMENTS

THIS AFTERNOON Judy stopped at the hospital to discuss funeral arrangements with Claire. She suggested a local funeral home for the service, a place with the heavy draperies, discreet lighting and folding chairs that funeral homes go in for.

"John wouldn't like that," Claire said. "Why not arrange a service at St. Cecilia's? It's a lovely church. The organist can play something from Mozart's requiem. And 'Nearer My God to Thee.'"

"'Nearer my God to Thee?' Would Dad want that?" Judy asked.

"It was never proved to your father that God existed,

if that's what you mean," Claire said. "Or that He didn't. It's what I would like." Claire grew up attending a charitable New England sort of church, and I never saw any reason to argue with her about her beliefs.

Judy backed off, and Claire didn't change her musical selections.

"Dad wouldn't want a regular funeral service," Judy said, "It should be informal. No clergy. It'll be a celebration of Dad, and a way to say good-by."

Good-by? Surely distinctions can be drawn, even though my body and I have parted company. *I'm here*, I whispered, sensing the hum of the Thread. *Can't you feel that, Claire?*

"Eric Wollmann and Deirdre Morton want to speak," Judy went on. The three of us had worked together to investigate psychics in islands of the western Pacific. Deirdre and Eric shun anything with an otherworldly smell, and they were vehement about the greedy fakers we found and eager to explain to people how they'd be fooled. But sometimes the victims only clung harder to their comforting beliefs. Often they were sad and bereaved folks, and I hadn't exposed their gullibility as fervently as Eric and Deirdre.

"I'll speak, too, Judy said. *There's my girl.* "And Greg will want to speak." Greg Lathrop had sometimes attended Skeptics' meetings with me, savoring the discussions and enjoying points of view he didn't always agree with. Greg is an attorney who could be a star in the State Department and can always find a way to get along with his wife, a woman of strong opinions.

24

He'd make a great dad, but after five years of marriage there are no kids; Claire and I wondered if working with the abused women and children at Home Safe had dampened Judy's interest in parenthood. Though it hadn't dampened our interest in grandparenthood.

"Some of the moms at Home Safe might want to come, too," Judy said. She is the chief executive at Home Safe, a non-profit providing shelter, medical attention and counseling for battered women and their kids. Claire volunteered at Home Safe, and I occasionally consulted when Judy had a question about the belief system of a client.

Judy is committed to her work; "zealous" might be another descriptor. She's expert at spotting abusers and their victims. A year ago, Claire and I were having dinner with Judy and Greg in one of the new restaurants on San Francisco's southern waterfront. Judy pointed out a young woman sitting a table or two away with an older man. The woman had a black eye, something that layers of makeup can't quite conceal. Judy followed the woman into the ladies' room and handed her a Home Safe Card, saying "Call this number when you need me."

My obituary appeared in the Sunday paper: "John Mason Court, well-known investigative journalist, died earlier this week in a devastating automobile accident that seriously injured his wife, Claire. Mason Court, as he was known professionally, was frequently honored for his investigations of paranormal frauds and

25

conspiracies."

"Mason" was my public persona, my career mask, the brick-and-mortar part of my name. Good-by to all that, I thought, the tatters dripping.

Today, the day of my funeral, I sat next to Claire in the front pew of St. Cecilia's, with Judy and Greg beside us. Deirdre Morton and Eric Wollman sat in the pew behind us, along with other members of the Skeptics Society. My body lay quietly in its coffin in front of the baroque altar framed by marble columns reaching toward the vaulted roof.

After trading glances at the opening chords of "Nearer My God to Thee," Deirdre and Eric praised their friend Mason's interest in getting to the facts, exposing false healers and dubious spiritualists. Judy spoke of how I encouraged her curiosity as a child, and Greg spoke warmly of our friendship.

As the organist segued into a closing hymn, a stranger appeared at the lectern, a sharp-eyed lean fellow in a glossy black suit. He opened a thin-leaved Bible and read in a voice that echoed among the pillars: "Save me, O God; for the waters are come in unto my soul. I am come into deep waters, where the floods overflow me. I am weary of my crying: my throat is dried: mine eyes fail while I wait for my God. Oh God, thou knowest my foolishness; and my sins are not hid from thee. . . I am become a stranger unto my brethren. . . Thou hast known my reproach, and my shame, and my dishonor: mine adversaries are all before thee."

The stranger stepped away from the lectern and walked stiff-legged down the aisle and out of the church. When the service ended and members of the Skeptics carried out my coffin, a dark bird flapped up from the church steps onto a telephone wire and peered down at us.

On the ride to the cemetery, I sat in the passenger's seat beside Greg. From the back seat with Claire, Judy demanded, "Who was that man talking about reproach and shame? How inappropriate. How could that apply to Dad?"

"Maybe it wasn't about your father," Greg said.

"You mean it was a mistake?"

"It might have been about somebody else."

Judy may have thought of Rick Mendoza then, because she sat up straighter and didn't say anything. For her, a scriptural reference lent my killer far too much dignity, and I completely agreed.

At the graveside, Judy put a red rose into Claire's left hand and laid her own hand over Claire's as the rose dropped onto the lid of the coffin. The tatters throbbed morosely as the body they'd been attached to settled into the fresh grave.

On the ride home, sitting in front beside Greg, I experimented with wall penetration. I couldn't get through the metallic layers of car door, but the window was open a crack, so I did the mouse trick and made myself super-thin. I slipped out between the door frame and the glass and found myself in the car's threatening jet-stream. Panicked, I squeezed back into the car..

CHAPTER 5: CLAIRE IN DANGER

TONIGHT Claire carried out the one-handed routine she learned in the hospital for cleaning the stump of her right arm and putting on a new dressing. She undressed for bed, sliding the nightgown past the soft brown mole below her right shoulder blade. She swallowed one of the three pills Dr. Hurd had prescribed and got into bed, automatically leaving room for me.

I slipped between the sheets, hoping to snuggle up and let my cool transparency be warmed by her dear shoulders and the sweet curve of her back.

Slurp. Flip. Flop. I slid out abruptly, kissed Claire good-night and stationed myself at the foot of the bed, sending her whatever calm I could.

She cried softly, her bandaged arm propped against

my pillow. After a while she fell asleep, and I wandered the room. Moonlight that drained her hair of color seeped through the curtains, and her nightmare filled the room. She woke, sweating and shaking, the lost hand calling out. The cloud of her pain sealed her off from me, and I retreated to the ceiling, cursing Rick Mendoza, criminally responsible for Claire's misery and our separation. The fact that he and I shared space in Claire's blood only made the feeling of separation worse, and my substance thickened with resentment.

Mallard appeared, wings fluttering in agitation: time for another meeting, *now*. We flew to McLaren Park, where Dog and Raven waited at the picnic table under a waning moon.

Raven spoke first. "You recognized me, didn't you? At the church. In the black suit?"

I nodded. "It was a powerful moment."

"And what did you think of those deep waters?"

"The deeper the better for the guy who drove the SUV. As soon as Claire testifies, he'll be doing time."

"Deep water for him, yes. And you yourself?"

I didn't see a connection. But Dog loomed full height before me. "You yourself: are you without reproach?"

I shared Judy's indignation about applying the Biblical mea culpas to me. Now Dog was pinning me with his eyes and suggesting exactly that.

All right. I rummaged around for old regrets. Once I dared my brother to dive off a dock into unknown water. He hit his head on something and nearly drowned. Luckily, an older kid jumped in and rescued him. I ran over a dog on the freeway, abandoned a pet turtle, watched a rabbit die of fright. I parted from a girlfriend I'd made half-promises to. I hardly saw my father after my parents split up during my senior year in high school.

Those memories stung. But surely they didn't match Rick Mendoza's list. The episode with my brother was part of growing up. And I didn't equate a dog's or a turtle's death, or the girl-friend thing, or even disappointing my father, with what killed me and cost Claire a hand.

"None of this," I began, "is in the same league with that."

But before they could hear me out, they looked at each other in alarm and vanished.

I returned to our house, where I found our bed empty, its sheets twisted, Claire gone. I sped along the Thread, which led me to St. James's Hospital, where she lay under an oxygen tent on the fourth floor.

"She has a high fever and difficulty breathing," Dr. Hurd told Judy and Greg. "We get that reaction when blood types don't match. But it's been days since her last transfusion."

Claire and I had the same harmonious "O" blood. But what about Rick Mendoza's toxic corpuscles?

Once again Mallard yanked me, as fast as portability allowed, to the hospital roof, where Dog and Raven waited beside the air conditioning intakes and exhaust pipes. Mallard set me down outside the circle of their exchange and joined them.

"He's still opaque. *Wrwwwkk.*"

"Uneducated," Dog said.

"Unaware, but not hopeless," Mallard offered. I caught an image of a duck in a shallow pond, barely able to stay afloat.

"He's a bother," Raven said.

"Bother is Opportunity," Dog said. "A bone, well buried."

"Maybe if she *dies*. That would be enlightening. *Quawwkkk.*"

"Wait a minute," I broke in. "Are you saying I'm responsible for what's happening to Claire?"

Dog sighed. "Come along now, or it will be too late."

The next moment Mallard and I were sliding through an open transom of the apartment in the Mission district where Rick Mendoza, the driver of the SUV, lived.

CHAPTER 6: FROM THE RECORD

I DIDN'T want to have anything to do with the SOB who killed me with his vicious driving and whose alien blood mingled with mine in Claire's bloodstream. "Why are you bringing me here? I should be with Claire."

"Stand back from all that," Dog said. "For your wife's sake."

In his room, Rick Mendoza, tall, lean, hard in the way of seasoned warriors and athletes--and also scruffy haired and smelling of stale beer--picked up a revolver, opened its chamber, took out the bullets, then put them back. The left side of his face was bandaged where there'd be a scar, and he limped when he crossed the room. He cursed the fact that he had fastened his seatbelt and so missed being die-pressed by the steering wheel or projected through the windshield and out of the looping memory of the accident.

Well, good enough. At least he has the sense to . . . I caught Dog's mind-reading glance. *All right, that's not what you brought me here for.*

The apartment walls faded into gray half-light, and I stood before an oval door with a green latch. As I lifted the latch, the door opened on scenes from Rick Mendoza's life.

He and his parents had left their native country in Central America when he was eight. I glimpsed frightened faces, heard the tattoo of gunfire. Running through the dark, hunger on a beach, a flashlight aimed on a path, then quickly switched off. More gunfire, more fear. Salt-flavored sea wind, an ancient boat limping north toward California, where seventy-year-old Omero Mendoza grew roses and lilies and azaleas in Schoonerville as the Mendozas had grown them for generations in their home country. He also grew the fir trees more suited to northern California and the Christmas tree trade. Omero welcomed Rick and his parents, who took over the business when he retired a few years later,

The child Rick found himself in an elementary classroom, surrounded with mysterious sounds which sorted themselves into American words. He soon coped with the language, with an accent the other kids seemed to hear first. He is reserved, teachers said. Takes his time about things. Doesn't cause trouble.

After school, he worked with his father to plant, prune and irrigate. Late in summer they sized up the next crop of Christmas trees, deciding which ones were ready to be cut down by the customers who came just before the big holiday.

At Christmas time, he helped his mother twist fir boughs around wire forms for wreaths and arrange holiday bouquets. In the glow of the whitewashed greenhouse she handed him a rose, smiling at him. *Go between the thorns.* Rick thought it might be his thorns that people saw and avoided.

A war was happening when he was 18. It was an exciting call to citizenship and bravery. He signed up for the Army, which put him through basic training and sent him on a barebones transport plane to Afghanistan. Six months of street fighting seasoned him in brutality. Then he was sent to a crude mountain outpost where survival of the platoon was a shared effort. Like Rick, the young men in his outfit enlisted at 18 or 19 or 20. Some of them would be cut down when they were not much older, the way Christmas trees were cut down when they turned a certain age. Rick recognized the rhythm.

On a moonless night, he and his buddy Dan reconnoitered on the rocky hillside below the outpost. A stone slipped under his boot and shouted their presence. Bullets arced toward them, and Dan lay beside him, bleeding his life away--in silence, not giving away their position.

A few days later, the outpost's firing killed five sheep in the valley below the outpost, where a village was wedged between the insurgents and the Americans. Rick went down with a small team to negotiate compensation for the sheep. They met with half a dozen village elders, who sat facing them on weavings which bore traditional designs, except for one in which a woven airplane dropped a woven bomb.

Through the platoon's powerful binoculars, Rick observed the villagers' activities. A beautiful woman, dark-haired and graceful in her movements, lived in one of the nearer houses. Through the door of her house he glimpsed a loom strung with warp threads and the beginning of a weaving. In decent weather, she came outside with an armful of wool that she carded and brushed into feathery rolls to be spun into yarn. Sometimes a baby ran in and out of the house and played in the dust by the faded shrub at the door.

At the outpost, another firing went awry, and the beautiful woman lay dead near the door of her house. The old men of the village sent up another demand for a meeting. They have a scale for these things, the lieutenant in charge of the platoon said, and again Rick went down with the Americans into the village, where the women and children stayed silent and invisible in their houses.

The "compensation" this time? The Record didn't say.

As Rick's life passed before my eyes, the present spliced into the past. During his time in Afghanistan,

Rick's father sickened and his parents moved to Arizona. When the Army discharged him, Rick came to San Francisco to live with his older sister Sylvia and her son, eight-year-old Charley. Sylvia had gone through a divorce a few years before and worked at a job combining bookkeeping and receptionist duties.

The night before our accident, Rick dreamed of the hillside blown apart, Dan's blood on his uniform, the closed door of the beautiful woman's house, the old men with their terrible eyes. In the morning, an email from a friend still in Afghanistan told him a buddy almost at the end of his deployment had been killed.

Rick pocketed the gun and took off in Sylvia's SUV, treading hard on the gas pedal. At the last minute, the light changed and our car headed into the intersection. *One more piece of shit to be gotten over with.* Rick floored the accelerator.

In Afghanistan he had survived unhurt, while friends in the platoon lay twisted and still and being alive felt like a betrayal. And now his remorse over what happened on a hillside in San Francisco darkened the Record.

If the universe is full of livable planets, there must be normal worlds whose inhabitants share an awareness of each other's suffering. Planets where they don't hate.

He killed me and ruined Claire's hand. Bottom line.

He lived through horrors that twisted him out of shape.. Bottom line there, too.

After Rick left the hospital, the Record showed that the judge made allowance for the Afghanistan vet with

36

his years of deployments and set Rick's bail low enough for Sylvia to manage. Charley, a bright-eyed kid, learned not to ask Rick too many questions. When Charley came home from school they ate peanut butter and crackers or a banana together. Charley loved to play Monopoly, and Rick tried to let himself care about the apartments on Park Avenue or the Boardwalk. Sometimes they shot baskets in the back yard or worked on the beginnings of a garden.

In the night, he woke shouting until Sylvia pounded on the door to the room he shared with Charley and he opened it to her anxious face lighted by the hallway globe. "How can we sleep? You'll wake up Charley." As he already had. He shouted at her, and she retreated down the hall. Back in the room, he opened the drawer and took out the gun and held it, cool in his hand.

The door to the Record closed. I was back in their room, and Rick was still standing in front of the open drawer palming bullets. I spied the Thread starting from Rick's solar plexus and heading in Claire's direction. Once again, my own segment of the Thread shook with resentment.

But what was I doing? Claire might die because my poisons were seeping into the Thread. I had to get a handle on this. I'd make myself watch the Record again, try to feel what he felt. I forced open the oval door to scenes from Rick's war. But the perspective had gone haywire; all distancing had vanished and I was devoured by the up-close experience of horror and loss, of wrecked bodies, of footsteps slippery with blood. I staggered away from the screen.

"Once is enough, dear," Mallard said. The door closed, and I was back in the apartment with Rick, who had closed the drawer. Rick's piece of the Thread still stretched into the night toward Claire, and I wondered how she would be affected if he killed himself, which seemed entirely possible. And understandable.

Had anybody thought of that?

And what about Claire herself? She spread her attention like a silken tent over stray dogs, pregnant cats, the kids at Home Safe, the abused women struggling with their histories. Her temper flared up at seeing women with purpled cheekbones and kids who clung and cried. She had every reason to be angry at the man who'd jammed my skull into his engine.

But she wasn't into hating per se.

Dog said, "The three of you are in this together. And you are the only one who is aware of it."

"Your attitude matters, dear," Mallard said.

"He has wronged you," Dog said. "Do not forget."

Small chance of that.

"You're connected to the Caring," Mallard said. "Remember that, too."

"Him? Remember? *Quarreekkwkk.*"

I felt split down the middle, gaping and empty.

Claire. Far off, a bell sounded her name.

Back at the hospital, Claire slept. She was out of danger, which puzzled Dr. Hurd. In the shadows of the room Dog watched calmly, Mallard sighed, and Raven

38

inhaled sharply, settling his feathers.

Later, the Animals and I watched a ceremony in the backyard of the apartment building, where his nephew Charley held in his hand a small brown bird, its feathers rumpled in death. Together he and Rick cleared a space and dug a hole, and Charley placed the bird in it. Rick was crying silently, his body shaking, while Charley covered the bird with handfuls of dirt and placed on its grave a few daisies that had sprouted in the yard. An earthy-muddy-oozy tatter detached itself from my substance and dripped onto the bird's resting place.

Rick heard from his court-appointed lawyer that his trial was scheduled for a date several weeks away. More waiting. He followed the news about the war on TV, exchanging emails on his sister's computer with a friend still at the northern outpost and another one at the command base on the plain. Nights continued bad.

CHAPTER 7: A WARNING

DOG CATCHES my longing to be in touch with Claire, and he eyes the Thread. "Communicating across the Boundary takes skill and experience," he warns me. "It's not for beginners."

"You're a fine beginner, dear," Mallard puts in. "But you'd only upset her."

I'm not so sure. Claire and I always talked things over. I was the one with a career in the limelight, the one who made the moves. But those moves took place after we talked. Before Deirdre and Eric and I went off to investigate another suspected spiritual fraud, Claire reminded me how people's faith, hope and love, even when mistaken and deceived, might contain some mysterious goodness that even they didn't understand. Remarks like that kept me from becoming too zealous.

So why can't I reach out to Claire and let her know I'm here? Why should that be forbidden?

The tatters are still hanging off my substance, pulsing with old longings and refusals, alongside the high-pitched hum of the Thread. Raven eyes a ripe shred and tears it off with his beak. *Ouch.* It wasn't ready to go.

Today we took a cab to the hospital, where Claire had an appointment with a physical therapist. The therapist brought out a device she called a mirror box: an arm-length wooden frame with a mirror fitted into one of its long sides and two arm-holes on the short side farthest from the mirror. Claire placed her arms through the holes so the mirror lay along what remained of her right arm. The mirrored reflection of her left hand gave the appearance of a right hand at the end of her sleeve. When she wriggled the fingers of her left hand, the hand in the mirror wriggled its fingers too. The hand raised a reflected glass and toothbrush, stirred a spoon in a reflected bowl.

From my perch on an exercise ball, I watched small whirlwinds of energy start up and particles of pain regroup themselves as Claire's missing hand found hints of meaning in the mirror, and threads in the torn fabric of her nervous system were picked up and rewoven.

"Even though your hand's gone," the therapist said, "your brain still registers phantom pain, as if the hand were still there. These reflections in the mirror of normal behavior can be reassuring to the lost hand."

Claire took the mirror home and practiced. When she turned her left hand palm up then down, the hand in the mirror echoed the change in sensation. Her left hand moved toward the mirror, its fingers gentle as they touched the reflection.

She leaned toward my empty armchair, rested the mirror box on it, and gave a mirrored pat, the beginning of a caress, which stirred quite a tingling in the Thread.

At Claire's next appointment the therapist said, "Since you've got most of your right arm left, let's try something more flexible." She brought out a mirror fixed to a wide elastic cuff to replace the unwieldy mirror box.

At home, with the mirror-bracelet fastened to the stump of her arm Claire sat at the piano and played scales, chords, and finger exercises with her left hand while the lost hand participated in the mirror. From the piano bench, she lifted out the sheet music for Ravel's *Pavane pour une infante defunte,* a tender piece with plangent chords moving in and out of harmony. I played the piano better than Claire, and as she hesitated over the chords, attempting them with the left hand, I felt how easy it would be to inject a little of my know-how, a hardly noticeable burst of energy, into her hand. But a shadowy nudge of Raven's wing intercepted the intention. And then a cautionary canine paw, and soft, admonishing quacks.

Okay. But the situation has to be more flexible. There has to be a chance for me to get in touch with Claire.

Holding a blue-marbled vintage pen from my collection, Claire sat at my desk and practiced writing with her left hand while the mirror reflected the moving hand. She opened my journal and read what I'd written just before the accident, notes on a case of spiritual fraud in which a medium deceived grieving parents who were paying large sums for messages from their dead child. With Claire, I read my comment: "Deception, and the resistance to seeing it!" Eric and Deirdre had exposed the medium, but the parents, hungering for evidence that their child's spirit lived on, continued to pay to be fooled. Dave and Deirdre took the attitude that "the truth will set you free," but it didn't always happen, given the longing of parents to communicate with their lost children.

Claire held my pen in her left hand and practiced writing, an awkward business with the non dominant hand. I wanted to help, and it was easy for my substance-arm to slip into hers. As I guided her hand, the writing smoothed and became even and sure. It was a chance to communicate, and the question I had formulated flowed from her fingers: "Aren't we always being deceived in one way or another?"

The handwriting with its firm t's and up-and-down stems looked like mine, and I heard a croak of dismay.

Claire stared at what she had written. "What's happening here?" she asked, her voice trembling.

In for a dime, in for a dollar. I ignored a warning growl and guided her hand to write. "And what do you want to know about what's happening?"

43

"What sort of question is that?" She gave her head a shake as if to clear it. "I'm not interested in turning into a Ouija board."

She put the pen aside and gave her left hand a shake, popping out my substance-arm. She worked with the mirror in ways she appointed for herself: fifteen minutes practicing the alphabet and numbers, fifteen minutes at the piano practicing scales in all the tonalities. Then she sketched for a while--the piano, the white orchid in the pot, the design of a rug she was fond of. She was getting better at using her left hand, and the atmosphere felt lively and alert.

That evening at the picnic table, there was a long uncomfortable (to me) silence.

Then, first up, Raven's croak: "'In for a dime, in for a dollar.' How whimsical."

Dog cocked his head. "Why have you interrupted your wife's healing?"

"I jumped in, I know. I was trying to help. I thought it would be stimulating." An unpleasant smell arose from the tatters.

Dog shook his head. "You have interfered."

"An occasional question might do no harm," Mallard offered, at which Dog glared at her and Raven shook imaginary dust off his wings. In the end, though, they didn't entirely forbid me to communicate with Claire. Maybe they can't, given our mingled blood.

I think I can improve my approach, if I continue to frame my remarks to her as questions. And if I make sure the handwriting slants backward, like hers. That

44

should help safeguard our relations.

Claire's interest in my papers is something we can share. It could be a comforting task for her to work on my unpublished   materials. If we stay close, linked by the Thread, our work together might   override the phantom pain.

Today I looked over Claire's shoulder as she opened the mail and saw the bill from the gastroenterologist for diagnostic services, $3500. "Our sympathy in your loss" had been hand-written underneath.

Dr. Erik Hammond came to the phone. "Ah yes, Mrs. Court. Please accept my sympathies. Not everyone wants to know the diagnosis when the patient has passed away from another cause, so in cases like your husband's we sometimes wait until there is a call."

Claire said she wanted to know.

"The tests were completely negative. Of course, given certain of his symptoms, we discussed pancreatic cancer as a possibility. He didn't mention that to you? In any case, there was only an incipient ulcer for which I would have written a prescription."

I hadn't wanted to worry Claire before the test results came in, though I expected the worst. Now I realized that if the accident hadn't happened, I'd be alive. I heard the brisk click of Mallard's bill, the croak of Raven, the sniff of Dog's nose. "Alive?" they repeated, the word shimmering in the air of This Side. Dog's mouth stretched wide in one of those contagious gulping yawns that lets in a big hit of oxygen. Then he leaped out of sight.

Later today, Judy came over today and filled Claire in on what was happening with the trial.

"In another month, you'll need to testify, Mom. Loud and clear."

"Loud and . . . ?"

"You'll be the star witness. A pedestrian saw your car move after the light changed, just before the collision, and he'll testify to that. But you'll be the main witness. It'll be up to you to be clear about what happened and what it's done to your life. And Dad's."

Claire said, "I don't feel ready, physically or otherwise. A month is too soon."

Judy hated to let things hang. But she said,. "All right, I'll ask Greg to get an extension."

Claire has textiles in her bones--women going back for generations who spun and wove, a grandmother who taught her to knit and crochet and had a loom on which Claire learned to weave. Not long after we moved to San Francisco, the De Young Museum had a major exhibit of nomad weaving from the Near East, weavings with designs tracing back hundreds, even thousands, of years. Claire saw the exhibit and wanted to weave again.

I built a simple frame loom for her and she worked at weavings that found a place in our house along with the tribal rugs and saddle-bags we picked up at dealers, and a whole shelf of books about nomad and village weaving in places like Turkey, old Persia, and Afghanistan. A weaving she began shortly before the

46

accident lay half-finished on the loom, with lengths of coppery red, gold, and blue yarn lying ready for knotting on the bench where she sat to weave. A design featuring twin dragons was pinned to the edge of the loom.

In the past, her hands worked together to wrap a length of yarn around two vertical warp strands, and then to bring the ends back through the space between the strands to form a knot, the smallest unit of a piled rug. But knotting required two-handed movements that her left hand couldn't manage. She tried flat weaving, no knots involved, and discovered that it was possible to weave with one hand. But it was slow and awkward. "Sometimes I need a hook," she told Dr. Hurd.

"Why not consider something more functional? Your right arm is ready to be fitted with a prosthesis, if you want one." But, despite the troubling pain, she didn't like the idea of a hook replacing the hand.

Raven quizzed me about the situation.

"There are things she could try, things she could manage with one hand. She might like to work on one of the projects I left unfinished."

"Concentrate on your research, using only one hand, requiring nothing more? *Quaererererkkkkk.*"

Tonight Judy and Greg took Claire to a play, a comedy that Judy thought would do Claire good, and I tagged along. The play was full of the long pauses comedians specialize in, after which anything, or nothing, that's said is hilarious. Judy, who had acted in

47

college productions, talked about "the beat," the moment of silent expectation that made the difference. "Break the silence too soon, or break it too late, it's wrong either way," she said.

Claire stiffened at that. She was back at the top of the hill as the light was changing and the SUV hurled toward us. When the light changed, had she edged out into the intersection a fraction of a second too soon?

When she brought up the question, Judy said, "Don't do that to yourself, Mom. Mendoza was in the wrong, and all you need to do is say so. You didn't run the light. He did."

"I could have waited a little longer."

"Please, Mom. You sound like one of the women in the shelter, trying to protect her abuser. Don't do that to Dad."

"Judy, I don't even know the man."

"Co-dependency works in strange ways, Mom."

"Co-dependency? Come on, Judy. There's nothing wrong with having a question."

"Well, it's a good thing you're not testifying today."

CHAPTER 8: A HAUNTING QUESTION

I KEPT ON fielding questions to Claire as she worked with my papers. It was easy to take charge of her left hand to write ambiguous messages. For a while she let this go on, seeming content to assign my end of the conversation to another part of herself which observed phenomena without fitting them into categories. So far, after their initial warning, Dog and his crew had not objected to these dialogues, except for a few muffled croaks and quacks.

Claire sorted through my notes, checking for

something to hand on to the Skeptics.

"What about John's music research?" she wondered.

My forearm entered hers, sensed the pulse at the wrist, the muscles and blood and bones beneath the skin, and guided her left hand to the mirror:

"Good idea. What do you think they'll find?" She understood that kind of questioning well enough, one part of her querying another part. Nothing to be alarmed about.

But I wanted to find a way to bring in Rick's situation, to hint at what I'd found out about him. So the hand added, "What do you know about him?"

"About who?"

The hand raced on. "What about the vet? The driver?"

"What about him? He killed my husband. I've lost a hand. He's been charged with manslaughter."

"But has he been convicted?"

"No, but he will be, or nothing will ever be right."

Something in me grunted "amen" to that, but the hand rushed ahead. "What if it looks different from another perspective?"

Except that everything blew up. Claire threw down my pen, expelling me from her arm. "Oh, shut up," she said to the mirror, tossed my notes onto the desk, and broke into sobs. She ran out of the room, slamming the door on the Thread.

Mallard, Dog, and Raven descended into the library.

"Oh, my dear," said Mallard. "What were you thinking?"

50

"Too many empty words," said Dog.

"An ulterior motive, perhaps? The not-so-small remains of your ego? *Quawwwwk*. Nipping might be needed." Raven eyed the trapped and fraying Thread.

Dog spoke. "*Haunting*. Is that what you want, to be a ghost haunting her?"

"I was trying to help."

"Help?" He held the word at paw's length. "Or *control*?"

I remembered how easy it was, in the human world, to equate "help" and "control" and "power." As Mason Court, I had written articles on the subject.

"You must work in another way," Dog said. "Try pictures, not words. They're all around you. Use them."

"I don't know how to operate that way."

"Learn another language. The wind blows, the leaves move, the trees sway."

Raven said, "Meaning comes from the sound of falling water. Or a bird's intelligent voice. *Quarrrk*."

"Now why should that be so hard?" Mallard asked. "You're quite capable, my dear. All you need to do is *listen*."

I got their point. Somehow my words weren't working. If I insisted on them, my connection with her would wither, or scare her into an illness she might not survive. The possibility of haunting her shocked me. I had read about what the Tibetans call hungry ghosts, lonely and greedy for power. Was I turning into a psychic amputee, still aching for my body's life the way Claire's arm ached for the lost hand? How much of

Mason's ambition still lurked in me?

And how much had I really wanted to communicate with Claire?.

Raven grukked, "Did it ever occur to you that you don't know much about your wife?"

"I think I know her pretty well. I love her."

Raven said, "Love. Whatever *that* means, now."

Who are these bossy creatures? Maybe my imagination has dreamed them up. On the other hand, who is this dreamer I call myself? For the briefest moment, the question brings a sensation of unseen wings behind me, covering the nape of my neck with their fluttering. Then they're gone.

I hadn't known that Claire kept a journal. This afternoon she took a notebook out of her lingerie drawer and leafed through entries, reading them while I looked over her shoulder. "John's work is important to him, and he's full of interesting experiences, and often wonderfully entertaining. He talked about his work non-stop all through dinner last night. There was no room for anything I said."

On another page she simply wrote, "And what about me? He never asks."

And, "How can I be lonely even when he is home?"

I remembered the times when I hadn't noticed, or asked, or listened. When I had talked and talked. .Something in me insisted on a defense: *It wasn't always like that. I did think of you. Didn't you notice? And were you always such an eager listener?*

52

Which seemed a fair response. Here were two people wanting each other's attention and not getting it. Neither of them quite wrong or quite right.

"*Wrong, right, right, wrong. . .Quawwrrkkkyukkk!*" .

Dog sends an image of two birds calling to each other in the forest, each bird listening while the other calls, then calling while the other listens. . . . And Mallard looks out at me from her wise, kind eyes.

I worry about Rick and the gun in the drawer. I wish I could arrange for the drawer to refuse to open, which would give him time to think before he picks up the gun and messes up his life and his sister's life and the kid's. And Claire's. But all I can do is follow and watch. Resent him and wish for him.

There's his drinking. He'll bring along a six-pack when he goes places with Charley, to the park or on the bus to Chinatown or Fisherman's Wharf. As they walk around, he'll take nips from the can or the half-bottle of merlot in its paper bag. I worry that he'll get careless about the traffic, that the wine will wear off and he'll let his inner scream loose on some stranger who bumps into him. I get mad at him then, in this odd remembering way that includes what I've found out about him.

Today he and Charley went to Ocean Beach, where the Pacific drags down from the shore with an undertow that regularly sucks in victims.

With towels and Rick's six-pack in a tote bag, Charley's beach bucket and plastic shovel, they scuffed through camel-colored sand until they found a spot above the high point of the rising tide. Rick spread out a towel, opened a beer, drank it, opened another. Charley dashed up and down the beach, running in and out of the waves and playing with a friendly dog.

Rick fell asleep on the towel, and I zoomed up and down the beach, hoping that people were keeping an eye out for kids. The tide was coming in, and a big wave could surprise Charley. But everyone was setting up umbrellas, or reading, or building sand castles, and no life guard patrolled that stretch of beach. Charley pranced in and out of the waves, moving farther and farther away from where Rick slept.

I hovered over Rick, hoping he'd wake up, my anger against him rising. How could he be so negligent?

A kid ran past and kicked sand in his face, and he woke up and couldn't see Charley anywhere. He sobered up fast, thinking of the washed-up body, the agony of telling Sylvia. Searching, he ran in the direction opposite to the way Charley had gone, calling his name. He ran toward a jeep proceeding in low gear along the packed sand, with two men in tee shirts and official-looking caps inside. "My nephew--have you seen him?" He described Charley, but the men shook their heads.

Then Charley bobbed up beside him, apologizing when he saw Rick's frightened face. He had gone all the way to Seal Rock at the other end of the beach. "You were asleep. I didn't mean to scare you," he said.

CHAPTER 9: McLAREN PARK

UNCE AGAIN Claire is taking the walks we took for years in McLaren Park, the second largest park in San Francisco. From the highest point in the park a water tower rises, painted a light blue that never quite matches the changing blues of the sky. Below the tower, primordial rocks edge Shelley Drive and circle a shallow pond where foot-long koi lurk. Mallards swim and mate, egrets and an occasional great blue heron silently watch for fish. On the slope above the water, crows frequent dark cypress trees. Dogs trot off-leash and dive into the pond to retrieve the balls their people launch from long-handled cups. Sometimes a dog swims after a mallard, who lifts off at the last moment, then splashes down at a safe but enticing distance.

It's late summer now and faded brownish-purple acacia pods litter the path around the pond. Earlier, before the accident, there were seven newly hatched ducklings, balls of light brown fuzz swimming nonchalantly in the pond, guarded by two adult mallards, a female and a male. Hawks circled high above the pond, and the count went down to six, then five.

Now there are three nearly grown ducklings left, still guarded by the brown-speckled mother and the male mallard. "We lose a few," Mallard murmurs.

I am feeling my way toward the shifting language of images and sensations that the Animals recommend. Words begin to lose a little of their hold. Maybe that's what Dog has in mind--seeing words as a gateway to the meaning that lies behind them. There are glimpses now of how everything consists of gestures: a cushion dented by Claire's arm; piano keys alert to being pressed; her left hand's quiet attempts at weaving; an orchid opening on top of the bookcase; a fern uncurling in our garden. In the park, the flight of a bird from pine to bottle-brush tree, or a bee's wriggle inside a blossom. Signs and omens. There's a delicate understanding that I keep losing and retrieving. In legends, the hero understands the language of birds after he gives up a hand or an eye. In small ways, I'm hearing tones of a different language.

This afternoon, as Claire and I walked around the pond, a lean whitish-yellow dog trotted toward us with a swift but arrhythmic gait, one of his hind legs missing.. Claire asked about that, and the dog's owner, a woman with graying hair and a kind face, told Claire she didn't know how he had lost the leg; he was a rescue from Hurricane Katrina, no details available. "He's happy to be here," the woman said as Claire stroked his lean shoulders and soft ears.

Back home, she whispered, "I'm lonely, John." She was sitting at my old desk, its light warming a photo of us taken with the dog we'd had years before. The light assembled itself in a halo around that image of our long-dead dog, a bright-eyed corgi. I hoped she'd notice that, and she did.

The next day Claire made a trip to the San Francisco SPCA, a state-of-the-art shelter for homeless animals, where tall glass windows look in on the generous spaces where rescued dogs live among sleeping pads, toys, and quilts. The sign on one window read, "Ashford: 12 years, 3 months old. Still wants a piece of the action. Loves long walks." Inside, a small black and white dog with upright ears and a confident tail allowed Claire to pet him. I knelt beside her and stroked him as he nuzzled against her hand. Claire took Ashford home, and he began shaping our living arrangements to his preferences, negotiating which sofas and beds and armchairs were suitable for the long naps he likes to take. He jumped up beside her on the sofa in the living room and snuggled against her right arm.

I couldn't help envying that little dog, the way his body went airborne with ecstasy at the prospect of a daily walk. The smells! The other dogs! How eager he was when his harness and leash appeared, tickets to the world he loved. And at home, with Claire feeding him, petting him . . . The Thread throbbed with envy and longing, Claire winced with pain, and I felt Dog's questioning eye.

Since the beach episode, I've kept an eye on Rick's drinking. Which he's still doing, but only when Charley is out with Sylvia, or sound asleep, or in school and he won't be seeing him for a while. Beer or no beer, the nightmares don't go away. And the gun doesn't stay in the drawer.

CHAPTER 10: DISCORD

DUANE ARUM, editor-in-chief of *Scrutiny*, the journal of the Skeptics Society, phoned Claire. The Skeptics wanted to honor me; could she attend their next meeting? They would show a film I made during one of my investigations and give me a posthumous award.

On the evening of the meeting Claire and I, along with Judy and Greg, arrived at the downtown office of Scrutiny in a darkened building of the financial district. The meeting room held seven or eight rows of chairs, which filled up with the men of a certain age the Skeptics attracted. Duane greeted Claire, Judy, and Greg, and ushered them to front-row seats.

My video showed a so-called psychic, a keen-eyed man, luring an audience into believing he knew something he couldn't have known. He had all the tricks –the rapid-fire questioning, the seizing of a promising answer by gauging the subject's feedback — the nods and quickening glances that gave him his next clue. Yes, there was a key of his in the drawer! Yes, coins in his pockets often came out in the wash! Once even a five-dollar bill. Yes, he did have a scar (the questioner running his fingers across his face, halting where the nod comes). Yes — on his right cheek at the jaw line.

All this was commonplace stuff. Until something changed.

The psychic, supposedly in contact with a recently deceased musician, was engaged in automatic writing on a large notepad. As the camera zoomed in on the hard-to-read scrawl, his hand veered into a large, precisely drawn symbol: a treble clef sign followed by a series of chords that passed from a minor key to variations of major chords and ended in a complex array of stacked notes not identifiable as either major or minor. Then back to the writing again, where "IMPROVISE" appeared in large letters.

The psychic did not attempt to nail anything down as "proof." He wasn't familiar with written music and did not attach any importance to the episode. It was hard to figure out its monetary value, something that often was not difficult. I thought that there must be dollar signs somewhere in this, even if I didn't see them. But the music intrigued me.

Duane said, "John wrote in his notes, 'This notation raises questions about regions of the brain specializing in musical relationships. Something unusual seems to be going on, some hard-to-identify shift in awareness.'" He said that James Adair, a neurochemist and one of our members, was interested in continuing this research.

"John would be pleased," Claire said. "I remember how he experimented with that music." I had played around with the chords the psychic jotted down, though the command to improvise didn't result in much, for the music seemed written in a code I couldn't crack.

At home after the meeting, Claire sat down at our piano and smiled when the notes she experimented with turned into "Green Sleeves." I perched on the arm of my old chair and listened to her halting playing. She took out the sheet music for Ravel's *Pavane* again and plunged into those difficult chords with her left hand. Discord reigned until it seemed even the Thread protested. My old urge to help appeared, I entered into her hand, and the music, now played accurately, filled with tender, pleasing grief. I entered her whole arm then, and the plaintive notes poured out of us as she swayed from side to side.

Her hand fell away from the keys, and Claire fainted, falling face down onto the keyboard. The Thread curled and hardened, trapping me against her. When I tried to pull away, something tore and Claire moaned with pain. I tried another tiny movement . . . Again, her cry stopped me.

Where were the Animals? But why should they come? They had warned me, a warning I had ignored. I tried another microscopic move. Again, the swift stab of pain.

All right. I'll be quiet. I won't move. Let the darkness have

61

me. But let Claire live. Please let her live, even if I never know about it.

"Sing." Dog's voice came from behind me.

"*Sing*. One note. Let it out. Now."

I obeyed, empty of anything except Dog's command, not knowing how my silenced voice could sing. Obeying anyway. Praying I'd be allowed to obey.

"O-o-o-o-o-o-ah-ahhhhhhhhhhhhhhhhhhh." The note, in a strong, midrange contralto, Claire's register, issued from her vocal cords.

The tight ball of the Thread loosened, her hand relaxed, and I followed the sound out of her body into the blessed air. She woke, stretched herself, raised her left hand to the keyboard and played a chord, not quite the one Ravel wrote, but beautiful. And then another.

I faced the Animals, expecting a reprimand or some isolating penalty.

Mallard said, "Lovely. Such singing."

Dog nodded. "Educational."

"It was a hard lesson," I said. "I'm not sure how many of those I can take."

"*Quawrrwwkk?*" Raven stared bleakly at me.

I paused. "Sorry. I'm not sure how many of those lessons Claire can take, either."

"Lessons," Dog said. "Yes. Painting lessons might be a useful for you."

"Painting? This image stuff is still beyond me," I said.

Raven looked bored. "Of course it is. Even more reason. *Craws.*"

"There's a knowing when something needs to be

62

understood," Mallard offered.

"I try to be well informed," I said. "But I suppose what you're talking about is different."

"Watch," Dog said. He loomed like an alert Cerberus, a guarder at the gate.

I watched him from a weary place. Cerberus wasn't speaking to me, so Dog returned to his own lean image, but with a face like mine, as if to say that if Cerberus didn't work he'd try something else.

.

CHAPTER 11: OPENINGS

AT THE ENTRANCE to the Arboretum in Golden Gate Park a single fir tree dominates the scene with its massive trunk and high, spread-out branches. A sketchbook of creamy matte paper floated up, along with a selection of drawing pencils, luscious graphite — 4B, 5B, 6B. I picked the darkest number and soon a drawing appeared that glowed with the life of the tree.

I wanted to go on, but Dog held up his paw.

"Do you really know what happened on the morning of the accident?"

"How could I? I didn't even know I was hit."

"Try to remember what happened just before that," he said.

I explored the painful memories that took me back to my place in the passenger seat of our car as Claire drove to Dr. Hammond's office, where he would give me the expected news that I was heading quickly toward the finish line. Sitting beside Claire, I felt tremendously sad to be leaving her. I relished the richness of our best moments together and regretted the times when I had phoned in my contribution. Was something possible in the little time we had left? I turned toward her and said, "Let's go somewhere, take a trip, wherever you'd like to go." She smiled at me and rested her right hand on my arm as we waited for the light to change.

The steering wheel was firm in her other hand, and as the light changed to green, she stepped on the gas pedal, almost as if that would get us to Hawaii sooner. But this was San Francisco, where you wait an extra second in case somebody starts through the intersection too far into the yellow light. Which was what Rick Mendoza was doing, aiming his SUV toward us.

As I've mentioned, Claire was usually late. The extra second was what she easily gave, gazing out the window at the children playing on the swings or the boy on his bicycle. But this time, caught up with what I was saying, she accelerated into the intersection the very instant the light changed.

Early, late--the timing's off, either way.

I had accepted the paramedic's assumption that Claire had automatically put her arm out to protect me, the way a mother reaches out to protect a child. Her gesture hadn't meant that, but it had been an expression of love, unique in its moment.

My last moment.

"Why do I have to see this?" I asked them, the tatters palpitating. "It hurts, you know." Dog reproached me

65

with a look, and I caught his drift; part of me lacked interest in what another part recognized as genuine. Didn't want to check out the fact that I was distracting Claire with words I couldn't wait to say. That my timing was off.

That I was responsible, too.

Occasionally Claire notices something I'm hoping she'll see, like the way the candle she lights sends its flame straight up unwavering. Or, when I suggest that the handspun wool by the loom invites her touch, she picks it up, holds it to her face and begins to weave.

If I concentrate on the mirror-bracelet as it reflects the images from Claire's remaining hand, a moment arrives when the amputated arm doesn't complain when the mirror image picks up a spoon or a comb or a pair of scissors. Even though the lost hand soon returns to its default of distress, I'm glad I felt that sweet pain-free moment.

I mull over what the Animals say about giving attention to a tree or a flower. But my best luck so far is with the mirror bracelet. And a piece of yarn and a candle. Am I the chief learner here? Claire has always been quick to receive omens. When it's time to change the subject, she knows it. She moves on to the next thing, which might be the wind tossing the branches of our pear tree, a cat leaping across the street, the taste of green tea in her cup, a child's upturned face. Meaning without explanation, or needing it. She has a natural talent for the language the Animals are trying to teach me, and her understanding of that is there when the waves of pain and sorrow subside

And she has Ashford, this little dog with a way of staring unemotionally in my direction, though he plainly adores Claire. He was twice left at the SPCA when previous owners moved, and he tenses into a ball of misery when something he counts on goes missing, like the rug in the hallway he crosses between sleeping areas: *She's taking it away like they always do just before they leave me.* When Claire saw that and put the rug back, he relaxed.

Watching him, it occurred to me that abandonment fits the situation of Claire's arm. It misses its hand and can't be comforted by the mirror.

"Abandonment? *Quarronnkkk.* I suppose the next thing you'll suggest is that her fingers are complaining about your abandonment to the afterworld."

I get Raven's point about self-pity. Still, the sense of abandonment isn't altogether about poor me. Someone else is crying somewhere. Is it my lost body, Mason moldering in his grave, or the tatters echoing his complaints? Or does the cry have to do with Claire?

Meanwhile, I look in on the apartment--at Rick shooting baskets with Charley, planting a few seeds with him in the fenced-in back yard, waiting for the postponed trial, feeling cooped up. His assigned attorney is busy with other cases and off-hand in his responses to Rick's questions. He tells Rick he can expect a sentence of at least several years, depending on the jury. Rick didn't drink the morning of the accident, but who can deny he was at the steering wheel of the SUV that killed me? He pleaded not guilty hoping there was something wrong with the SUV, but no defective brake or steering wheel has been found.

Rick is a mess, haunted by years spent on the edge of annihilation. As far as I can tell, his kind of mess isn't making Claire sick, the way my hate for him had. Maybe he's turning the hate back on himself. Which isn't a healthy thing to do, even if it leaves the Thread unpolluted.

I pointed out to the Animals that Rick seems willing for justice to be done by serving prison time. I mentioned the scare on the beach and its continuing good effect

"He now has a rudimentary understanding of the Law of Consequences," Raven croaked. "Ru-di-men-ta-ry."

Dog nodded. "When it rains, the sidewalk gets wet. He understands that."

Mallard said, "It's enough to begin. That's splendid."

"You're suggesting what?" I asked.

Mallard pointed her beak north.

I still worry that Claire's unhappiness about my death and her resentment of Rick will sicken her. Taking charge of the pen with leading questions was my way of working on that, even though I screwed up. I am willing to try the new wordless imaging. But often I can't help highlighting a word Claire is reading in the newspaper — "peace" or "forgiveness."

"Be subtle," Raven urges. "Why do you still trust

words so much?"

Dog says it in his own way. "How to leave a mark where it is needed? Can you take the chance your message won't be understood?"

"Coincidences. Timing. The unattainable carp." Mallard means the bulky orange and off-white presences in the pond at McLaren who seem to defy all efforts to turn them into dinner. Some things aren't readily available, or need to be.

Something in me is more alert, and I'm wondering what else might be possible. Are there opportunities I haven't considered? Tiny ways to influence the perception of meaning? Today the wind parted branches and a sun-ray fell on a ridge of cypress bark into which a shred of newspaper bearing the word "love" had tucked itself. More reliance on words, I know. But the word was there to be seen, and Claire saw it as she bent to fix Ashford's harness and a fresh breeze from the Pacific parted the morning fog and opened the view all the way to the Farallones. Pebbles scattering into a constellation, a white feather drifting down, islands appearing out of the sea--omens are constantly arriving, blazing with wordless meaning.

These words flow from my ghostly hand onto the ghostly page of this notebook. What I write mostly masks the meaning, but sometimes a different life gleams through the words.

Today Claire and I visited my grave, where a small granite marker bore the words: "John Mason Court,

69

1964-2016." The afternoon sun shone brightly on all three words of my name, not discriminating against old Mason. Nearby, large memorial stones made Wagnerian gestures, pledging eternal remembrance and reunions in paradise. I was struck with the simplicity of the stone Claire had chosen and its roseate sparkle, and did my best to offer her that impression.as we knelt together while she arranged the chrysanthemums she had brought.

Claire didn't notice, and when I found that hard to bear, she shivered a little as if she had taken a chill. Above us, at the edge of the cemetery, a row of slender firs twisted around their centers, not quite touching each other.

CHAPTER 12: GONE

THIS AFTERNOON Claire came home, weary after working her way through quiche and salad while Judy tried to persuade her to file a suit against Rick Mendoza, saying he should be made to share costs. He's probably penniless, Claire said, but she'd think about it.

As she came into our house, the phone was flashing: "Mrs. Court, this is Rick Mendoza's sister, Sylvia Martin. Please call me. Rick is gone."

I sensed the "no" of resistance rising in Claire. *Nothing doing.* She wouldn't call back. She went to the kitchen and poured herself a glass of water, choked on it, coughed, and struggled for breath. Ashford trotted up, curious. She sat down at the table and picked him up and held him, caressing his soft ears and the white patch on his chest. His sturdy body settled into her lap, and she relaxed.

She went back to the phone. "Claire Court, returning

your call. But why wouldn't I be the last person you'd want to call?"

"I saw your picture after the accident and felt connected. I need someone to talk to."

Claire remembered how the mothers at Home Safe exchanged stories of their experiences. She and Sylvia shared the same story.

"All right, I'm listening."

Sylvia said that when she came home from work the day before, Charlie was playing a computer game by himself in the living room. He hadn't seen Rick. "We were going to do stuff in the back yard," he said. "Stuff" meant shooting baskets and tending the small garden they had planted.

Sylvia found a note from Rick saying not to worry, the trial was delayed again and he was taking off. He needed to get away. Charley, do your homework. The bureau drawer where he kept the gun was empty.

She told Charley that Rick would be away for a day or two.

"He didn't take his gun, did he, Mom?"

"I'm not sure. He might have hidden it." But Rick was still gone the next day, and Sylvia called Claire. "I haven't told anyone else," she said. "I keep thinking Rick will be back tonight, or tomorrow."

Claire remembered loss and its needs. "Can you and Charley come over?" Almost immediately, a huge "no" rose in her. But Sylvia had already said yes.

They arrived an hour later--Sylvia small and dark-haired, and Charley, a solemn eight-year-old. She and

Sylvia sat down together on the sofa, while Charley petted Ashford, who ignored an offer to play catch with a rubber ball. "You'll have to put up with him," Claire said. "He does one thing really well, which is to take me on a long walk every day. He likes to eat, too."

"Are you the lady who lost her hand in the accident?"

Claire nodded. "My arm is almost healed now, and I can choose a new hand, if I decide I want one."

"Can I see how it works when you get it?"

"If I get one, you can help me figure it out." Charley went off to work on Ashford's relationship with the rubber ball.

Claire turned to Sylvia. "How much does Charley know?"

"I told him that Rick was involved in a terrible accident and how bad he felt about it." It was enough of the truth.

Sylvia told of Rick's return from Afghanistan, the nightmares, the fits of anger, the drinking and its lessening. His fondness for Charley. He'd been in contact with his mother in the Southwest, but it was hard for her to understand what he was going through. Sylvia didn't think that Rick would head south; he still felt connected to the north coast.

Charley came and sat beside his mother. "Check your messages, Mom. Maybe there's one from Rick."

She swiped her phone. "Nothing yet."

"That could be good news," Claire said. "He might not want to be found."

73

"He might be hiding? Do the police want to find him?"

"I don't know, Charley. I hope not."

"He could be on his way home," Claire said. "He'll be missing you."

"Let me know when you hear something," she told Sylvia as they left. "Why don't you bring Charley over on Saturday? Ashford and I will show you around McLaren Park."

After they left, Claire sat down in our study, feeling the shock of their visit. She had let them come, in the face of the fact that Brother/Uncle Rick was responsible for my death, and for her missing hand. The thought of Rick closed her down, and she wanted to take back the whole afternoon. I have remnants of my own attraction to that attitude, but the filament pulsed, reminding me of Claire's bloodstream and my important place in it. I watched with her till her reaction calmed.

Even then, Raven didn't miss a chance. "Your important place? *Quarrkkkwwkk.*"

All right. Mostly self-important. But didn't my attitude matter?

Ashford trotted into the study, campaigning for a walk, and the three of us headed up the Peru street steps with its trees and wild flowers to McLaren Park and the duck pond. The fog had burned off and the late afternoon sun shone on the water. Soon a stiff wind from the Pacific would bring back the fog already glowing white offshore. Crows careened in the drafts above the pond, playing with each other and the wind. Two of them rose above the cypresses, one lunging in midair for the other, the other feinting away, then skillfully returning the lunge. Claire looked up and wondered whether they were playing or dancing or fighting. Finally, the crows entered the same trajectory, one following the other until they flew out of sight.

Though Rick was in big trouble with the California court system, Dog did not dwell on that. "Follow him north," he told me. "Keep an eye on him."

"What about my connection to Claire?"

"By following him you won't be losing touch with her."

"It's always the remembering that's needed," Raven said hollowly, "and it's always forgotten."

"All right, I'm supposed to remember, but what exactly does that mean in my situation?"

"Sometimes I wonder why we bother. They all forget, even here. These days they come to us without even the Basics."

Dog frowned at Raven and he shut his beak, muttering something about "missing connections."

For a moment, I was back in the chapel, listening to the words of the figure in black, struggling to understand a situation that went deeper than I could grasp. What connections was I missing? I'd seen something of my anger with Rick; I'd spotted that and was working on it, for Claire's sake. Maybe also for his. There were those mistreated animals from my youth. And the girl friend who moved on and probably found somebody a lot more suitable.

Then there was family stuff.

My parents were a mismatched pair of lace-curtain Irish and farm-folk German; after years of arguing, they split up the year before I graduated from high school. When my father received a family inheritance, he made his move. He left my mother the inheritance income, quit his job on the local police force and moved up north to hunt and fish and manage a small resort. When I was younger, he had tried to interest me in the outdoors life he loved, but my fishing line tangled and I didn't like guns. He didn't insist, just kept on making fishing and hunting trips with his police-force friends. In 1984, I received a scholarship to UC and dived into science and psychology courses while working on the campus newspaper, which gave me ideas about using my split major in the journalistic area.

After college, there'd been the pressures of building a career and starting a family with Claire, and I didn't see much of my father in those years. Once or twice I got into his part of the state while on an investigative trip for *Scrutiny*. Something in me complained that he hadn't stuck around. If he wanted to see me, why couldn't he come for a visit?

When I was small, for several weeks every summer we rented a cottage halfway around a small lake in Michigan. When my father worked during the week, on Friday night he drove up to the cottage. Rounding the lake, he tooted the horn of his car to a beat I listened for eagerly.

"Shave-and-a-haircut. . .two bits!!"

I loved the rhythm of that and the pregnant pause just before the burst-out at the end. The oiled gravel of the road crunched as he pulled up in the Malibu and I was lifted for a hug and a piggyback ride.

My mother liked city living; after she and Dad split up she stayed in San Francisco, where Claire and I visited her often until she died of cancer ten years ago. When my father died suddenly three years ago, I attended his memorial service, flying up north with Claire, sitting in the white framed funeral home in the small town. For a few days, I was hit hard by the sense of how a life goes on and then is over. And that it's the same for all of us.

On September 11, 2001, the same truth--that we're all going to die and it can happen any time--was evident to everyone in the country, and, for a little while, there was a re-sorting of priorities. People felt moments of tenderness, even toward strangers. But that passed, and even my own death didn't empty me out in quite the same way.

"I have hopes of remembering," I told the Animals. "Please don't give up on me."

"Silly in-between one," Mallard said. "Giving up on you is not in the picture."

Which for some reason made me feel brave.

CHAPTER 13: THE LETTER

THREE DAYS after Sylvia came over, Judy called. "Mom, Rick Mendoza has skipped town. I checked with the police today. He's been gone several days. He left a note that didn't say much."

"Did he say where he was going?"

"Well, of course not!"

"What's the point in suing someone who's left the scene and not mentioned where he's going?"

"The lawsuit can wait. Greg doesn't think there's much hope of gaining anything from Mendoza, anyway. Somebody needs to find him, and if the police don't locate him soon, we should hire a private investigator."

"Just when I was trying to get on with my life."

"Mom, you *can* get on with your life. Let Greg and me handle that. There has to be justice for Dad."

"All right. But be careful."

"Careful? Well, of course, Mom. Or . . . are you suggesting we should get protection? That the vet might be a stalker?"

The police told Greg that: they were doing everything they could to find Rick Mendoza. They had sent out an All Points Alert, with multiple agencies notified. There were indications of his whereabouts which they could not disclose, and it was better not to interfere as they pursued their investigation. Greg was invited to check in now and then.

At this point, Home Safe began its yearly appeal for money, and Judy's job took over her life as she plunged into photo shoots, press releases, speaking engagements, and phone calls to prospective donors.

And then, tucked into the scabby bark of an umbrella pine near the pond at McLaren park, I found a letter. Folded to make its own envelope, the letter looked as if it had come out of a pack of colored construction paper. "To God" was printed on the outside in big childish letters.

"Read it," Raven said.

"It's not addressed to me."

"For sure. But finding a letter like this means that you can read it."

I'd written a letter to Santa Claus once and received a friendly reply postmarked North Pole which delighted me: somebody up there had noticed me. Years later I found out that a post office in Indiana engages in benevolent deception, but I still liked the idea.

"Read it to me," Raven said. Mallard came close and Dog's ears were antennae.

"Dear God, please help mama find me. Love, Elena"

"I think I already know about this," I said. "It happened two years ago. And Elena's dead."

Maria, the woman with the black eye that Judy spotted in the restaurant, was married to Arnold Warp, the owner of a chain of dollar stores. A clever immigrant's push for position and wealth earned him an address in Pacific Heights to which he brought Maria as his bride from the home islands. Her parents were acquainted with Warp's family, and when Warp came courting, the beautiful young girl was attracted to the dignified, handsome older man, while her parents approved the wealthy businessman well able to care for their daughter.

After a lavish wedding and a honeymoon in Hawaii, they settled into Warp's opulent home in San Francisco. A year later Elena, now four, was born. The recession arrived, and Warp saw his assets dwindle. He took out his fear and distress on his wife and increasingly on their daughter. Soon he claimed that Elena was not his child. Maria was a whore who betrayed him with who knew how many men? A few weeks after we'd seen them in the restaurant, he attacked Maria again, beating her on the breasts and stomach. That night for the first time his belt lashed out at Elena.

The next day Maria drew the Home Safe card out of hiding and called Judy.

"You've got to get out of there, you and Elena. Now.

Walk out. Give me your address and I will be there in fifteen minutes."

"All right, but my husband is on his way home. He will be angry if I am not here to meet him."

"So that he can abuse you and your daughter? Take Elena's hand and walk out the door."

On her cell phone Judy heard, "Come with me, Elena, we need to mail a letter."

"Is it a letter to God, mama?"

Near the mailbox, Judy sat in her car, the doors unlocked, the motor idling, as the mother and child approached. A black BMW rounded the corner, with Arnold Warp signaling his driver to intercept the two figures running toward Judy's car. Maria and Elena scrambled in, the door slammed and locks clicked into place as Judy frantically backed away from the Beemer.

"Follow them, sir?" Warp's driver gestured. But Warp cursed and shook his head. It wouldn't do for a Pacific Heights landowner to be apprehended for chasing down a fleeing wife covered with bruises. Judy swerved past the black sedan and sped down Broadway.

Maria and her daughter came to Home Safe, where they found refuge in a high room with a view toward the Golden Gate Bridge. Arnold Warp was issued a restraining order that forbade contact with them, and life settled down for the mother and daughter. Elena was taken each day in the Home Safe van to the nursery school she'd been attending, was later picked up and returned to Home Safe from the school's isolated location deep in Eagles Park ravine.

One morning, as the children played outside, a watching mother was distracted. The next time she counted the children, one child, Elena, was missing. One of the children said, "Her brother came for her, or maybe her daddy." After a few days' search, the child's strangled body was found, deep in the ravine. Arnold Warp, though the primary suspect, had been out of the country on business when Elena was kidnapped, and he denied any connection to the abduction and murder. His wife had left him, a divorce was in the works, that part of his life was finished. Why should he kill his own child when he was fighting for the right to see her? And so on. Rumors of "foreign" gangs increased internet hits for a few days, then evaporated, unverified.

Judy protected Maria, defending her against reporters and photographers eager for details of her marriage. Through friends elsewhere in the state, she found a place far out of the city where Maria would be safe and could begin to recover. "I don't want to know exactly where she is myself," Judy told me and Claire.

At the time, I tied Elena's death to certain practices of black magic in his home island. But I had no proof and no time to investigate. What was the meaning of this note from a dead child?

"Am I supposed to answer this?" I asked.

Dog's nose quivered, Raven's head tilted in query, Mallard hummed tunelessly. And the letter had vanished.

CHAPTER 14: THE SUPPORT GROUP

THERE'S a coffee shop in the Excelsior with comfortable chairs and polished oak tables and cinnamon rolls from the best bakery in nearby Noe Valley. Claire likes to go there in the morning. On a bulletin board near the entrance people post offers of services--reiki sessions or pet sitting or practice your English.

Today the board announced an "Amputee Support group," giving a phone number like ours, an Excelsior number starting with 382. Before long Claire walked over to the board and read the notice.

She called the number, and Edith, the woman who answered, said the group was for people who had lost a limb and were dealing with phantom pain and all the other adjustments. It wasn't a professional therapy group, just people with similar experiences. Claire was welcome.

Two days later Claire rang the bell at the door of a house on Edinburgh Street, not far from our house.

The door opened to a pale yellow dog wagging its tail. The dog had only three legs, and the woman beside him, smiling in recognition, was the woman we had met in the park weeks before.

Three others were there: Don, a wiry man of 25, had lost most of his left forearm to in a battlefield explosion in Afghanistan. His arm had been replaced with a slender metal pole that ended in a steel gripping device. "Hi there, lefty." He shook Claire's hand with his own remaining hand.

On the sofa Francie, a pretty, heavy-set woman in her forties, said that her left leg was amputated below the knee and that she walked with an artificial limb. "It's from the diabetes," she said. Edith's son Jeff, about 20, slumping in a chair, had lost his right arm, well above the elbow, in a motorcycle accident three months earlier. He didn't register Claire's presence and pushed his chair back when the others drew theirs in to make a circle.

Claire launched into a quick summary of her situation, mentioning the accident, the loss of her husband, the loss of her right hand, the phantom pain. "I'm interested in what I can do with this mirror," she said in a bright voice, bringing the mirror-bracelet out of her handbag. "I'm trying this out and could use some advice."

"Otherwise everything is under control? You just need a little help with one of those cute mirror things?"

"Easy, Don," Francie said.

84

"Sometimes we're a little rough on each other." Edith looked mildly in Don's direction.

"She's trying to be polite about my PTSD," Don said. "Of course, nobody wants to admit they have it, not even the guys who wake up screaming at night and shake all over when a car backfires."

"It's about the pain, at least for me it is," Francie said. "My left foot still wants to wiggle its toes, and that can give me a hard time. The mirror thing helps sometimes."

Edith asked Jeff if he had anything he wanted to say. His forehead seized up and he shook his head. "He's having some bad nights," Edith said.

"Tell me about it," Don drawled.

Claire said, "I have these horrible dreams about the accident. I don't know if I'll ever want to drive again."

Don looked at her as if he hadn't seen her before. "Driving could be a way off. When you're ready to buy a car, have a knob put on the steering wheel and you won't even need one of these." He glanced at his prosthesis. "It's pretty easy to drive when you're one-handed. Though Captain Hook here is a great invention."

Edith brought out coffee and home-made cupcakes. "Mirrors might be an idea for next time," she said. "And why don't you bring Ashford? Mitzi likes company."

Claire went into my study and opened a drawer and took out something she'd known was there but had not wanted to look at: a picture of the three of us taken when Judy was little and we were on vacation, relaxed and happy at a Sierra campsite. She let herself cry, then got up and went to the refrigerator and figured out what the left hand was going to help her cook for dinner.

At the next meeting of the support group, Claire told of getting up the courage to look at the picture and the tears that followed. Don told how it tore him up to think of the friend who'd been killed beside him in the incident which cost him his arm.

Claire said, "The driver of the SUV that hit us has been charged with using a car as a lethal weapon. Vehicular manslaughter."

"That's a mouthful," Francie said.

"My daughter is thinking about suing him."

"Go ahead, sue the bastard," Don said. "It'll distract him from his other problems." The room fell silent. "Sorry, not funny. A friend of mine was back a whole year, and one day he came up against the wall one time too many, went into the garage and shot himself."

"Why didn't I die? Why not? What's the point of being like this?" Jeff hit his stump hard against the table.

"Don't talk like that, honey. Please," Edith said.

Francie said, "You mustn't worry your mother. You have a lot to live for. There are people who've lost both arms, or both legs, or all four limbs, and they're doing fine. I've seen the most wonderful paintings, and the artist did it with his mouth or his foot." She was on a roll.

"You know what helps me?" she asked. "When I'm feeling bad I switch over to thinking about all the things

I'm grateful for right now, everything I can see and hear and touch. Right now. Looking at all of you, glad that Jeff is here, thankful to Edith for opening her house, thankful for my left leg, thankful for as much of the right leg as I've got."

All right, I get the idea, some part of me protested. But Claire was listening to the sound of Francie's voice, direct and quiet, and the Thread was vibrating calmly.

The next time the support group met, people came with mirrors they strapped to a remaining leg or arm. Jeff used the mirror box as Edith, bubbling, whispered that he wouldn't bother with it before.

Francie took off her right shoe and let her pink-lacquered toes wriggle in the mirror. Don was equipped with an armband-mirror like Claire's. Edith made a high-sign in Don's mirror, and he grinned and went over to Jeff, reached out his long left arm and hand, waved fingers in the air and in the mirror, and got Jeff to grinning. Jeff wiggled a foot in Francie's mirror, and Francie waggled her pretty right foot in Claire's mirror.

They laughed a lot, and the dusty depressed one in me challenged their laughter. What did they have to laugh about, really? At that, the filament throbbed hard.

"I don't sleep well," Claire told Dr. Hurd. "I wake up in a sweat after these dreams about the accident. Mostly it's the awful sound. Things are exploding around me and then I'm swallowed up in the dark. When I finally get back to sleep, the dream comes again.

And the hand hurts."

Dr. Hurd gave her a prescription which, being Claire, she wanted to ignore. But after hours of sleeplessness she took a tranquilizer, felt numbed by it, yet slept better. These things are never straightforward, she told herself.

When she mentioned tranquilizers in the support group, Edith said, "After Jeff's accident I couldn't sleep, and I took tranquilizers for a while. I've still got some in the medicine cabinet. I like to know where they are."

Don said to Claire, "Those dreams can get to you. You can be sure the other driver has it in spades. It took you a few bad seconds to have a taste of it; he had two or three years of a lot worse. And after what he did to you and your husband, he's got dreams all right."

"I think I'm partly to blame." Claire tried that out on the group. "The light had hardly turned green. I keep thinking about what might or might not have happened if I'd waited a little longer. Or if the car had stalled out."

"Right," Don said. "You feel like you did something, or didn't do something that would have made a difference. "You made a noise on patrol that gave their life away. They would have given their life for you, and you gave theirs away. We all get dishonorable discharges."

"When you think along those lines, you do," Francie said.

"This support group is fine for Claire," I told Raven, "and I'm glad for her, but what am I supposed to do with myself? Suddenly I don't fit in anywhere.

Communicating with Claire is limited to trying to attract her attention nonverbally. Try that when you're invisible. She's busy with all these new people. If I have a job to do, I can't see what it is."

Mallard and Dog appeared, and Raven filled them in. "He thinks he's out of work," he told them.

"You don't have your Post yet," Mallard offered. "One's task changes of course, but with a Post--there's always something to do."

Dog said, "For now you'll have to settle for unemployment, or what looks like it."

"I don't like being without an assignment," I told them. "An investigation, or a problem to solve." Dog sent me the image of a night sky full of gazillions of burning, unanswerable questions.

"And who can bear not having an answer?" Raven cawed. He seemed to find the situation amusing, but my fragile connection with Claire frightened me. By being dead had I become obsolete and powerless?

However, my companions were having none of this, and Raven's amused laughter and Dog's clear gaze helped me to question my fears, so for a little while I was free, naked, and safe under the brilliant sky.

Then the urge for certainty returned like an itch. What was my role in all of this? How was I needed? What was this "post" the animals spoke of? What did the blood connection threaten, or leave me vulnerable to? What was I still forgetting?

"If you're not telling me something," I told them, "I'd appreciate hearing about it. I'm used to specific goals."

Mallard said, "We'd tell you if we could. I'm sure it's for the best, dear."

"Or you'd experience it if you could," Raven added. "In fact, you just did." I looked then and saw that the sky-view was gone. And I realized I'd forgotten Rick.

CHAPTER 15: RICK'S JOURNEY

RICK HITCHED rides up the coast, heading toward Schoonerville, saying when asked that his relatives used to have a Christmas tree farm there. His last ride out of Redding landed him in the town of Fortuna, not far from the coast. Leaving the roadside restaurant where he had a cup of coffee, he shouldered his pack and stepped toward the highway.

A pick-up truck turned out of the parking lot, and Rick signaled for a ride. "I'm going in the direction of Schoonerville," the man with quiet eyes said. "You're welcome to ride with me." Rick climbed into the passenger seat beside a lean man with a trimmed blond beard.

"You're maybe looking for something up this way, or going back to something?"

"I used to be from here before I went into the

service."

"Looking to make a fresh start?"

Rick nodded, and the driver said, "Fresh starts aren't always easy."

Rick could only agree, and they fell silent together.

Around a bend in the road, Rick spotted regular rows of fir trees, young to adolescent to mature, Noble and jack and northern pine. A driveway led off the road, where a sign read "Harry's Christmas Tree Farm. Drive in and cut your own." It was Mendoza's Christmas Trees in his father's day, and the painted-in "Harry's" stretched out to cover the space.

He got out, thanked the driver, and received a parting "good luck."

Near the road, a man was closing a tool shed. "You say you came here as a kid? Then you knew Martin Mendoza."

Rick nodded. "My uncle. I used to come here in the summer and work for him."

"So, you're old Mendoza's nephew. What do you hear from him?"

"He died last year. He and my aunt had moved to Arizona for his health."

"Sorry about that. He was a fine man. Almost every day I walk around the property and see where he repaired a fence or put in raised beds in a place where you wouldn't otherwise be able to grow anything."

"I helped my uncle with some of that."

"People around here still mention your aunt's floral arrangements. What about you? Continuing the family work?"

"Those were good times. I'd like to think so."

"You're lucky to have people who gave you a start. Looking around the area for something, are you?"

"Just passing through." A woman with faded blond hair walked up the path from the house and looked hard at him. "Do I recognize you?" she asked.

"Most likely, Betty," her husband said. "Martin Mendoza's his uncle, or was."

"There's a family resemblance all right. You look a lot like him."

"People used to tell me that," Rick said. The woman turned away then, but the inquiry didn't leave her face.

He caught another ride in a truck heading out of Schoonerville. The driver said he had an overnight delivery to make, and if Rick rode with him he'd be dropped off in the boondocks where nights were chilly. Rick said cold weather camping suited him fine; he had a small tarp and a sleeping bag in his backpack.

The man let him off on the main highway and headed his truck down a gravel road.

Rick watched while the truck drove a hundred yards to a wrought iron gate set between stone pillars. The gate opened, the truck drove through the entrance. Rick realized that he had arrived at a place familiar by reputation from his childhood--the Adams estate, old man Adams's kingdom. Memories poured in of stories he'd heard of the old man and his penchant for privacy and what people called "preservation," a term that hadn't meant much to him then. As the gate closed, Rick caught sight, in the deepening twilight, of a human form standing beside one of the stone posts framing the gate.

After the rumble of the truck faded, he walked up to the gate and found it locked. He shook the gate hard. But whoever had been there was gone.

Chapter 16: The Silver Hand

THE THREAD vibrated, and I found myself back in San Francisco, where Claire was having an intense conversation with Judy.

"Of course, I can drive," Claire said. "The physical therapist said people drive all the time with one hand. I've got almost my whole right arm to help, and I can have a knob fixed to the steering wheel so I can turn it with my left hand."

"Mom, I'm not sure you should be driving at all. A knob might work for getting around the block in a city which is level, but not in San Francisco." The physical therapist had questioned that, too, Claire remembered.

"I thought I'd try to get along without one of those hooks."

"Are you referring to something that could actually grip a steering wheel?"

"They're ugly. What's left of the right arm is getting

better at helping me balance."

Ugly prosthesis, ugly hook, the phantom hand wailed.

"Mom, if you were sick and the doctor prescribed an antibiotic, you'd take it to get better, wouldn't you?"

Claire remained silent.

"No, I suppose you wouldn't," Judy said. "I think you're being stubborn."

Claire made an appointment to talk things over with Dr. Hurd. The mirror box and bracelet were a help, she told him. But the phantom pain was still there. "Maybe it knows I'm trying to fool it. Making up things for it to pretend to do, then pretending it can do them."

"What would you like your hands to be able to do that's not imaginary? What did they do that they can't do now?"

"I'm sure I could learn to drive with one hand. Writing is getting easier with the left hand. I can cook with one hand. But I want to weave, and weaving doesn't work well with one hand. Certain things, like knotting, I can't do." It was the clearest she'd been.

"Weaving? Terrific. May I suggest something? Would you consider an appointment with a specialist to discuss an artificial hand? You could start with the simplest kind. It won't look like a real hand, but it will be easy to learn to use and you'll be able to pick up things, hold a pen or a spoon or the threads of your weaving."

Captain Hook, Claire thought. The sinister, mechanical look of those things. But she wanted to weave. She'd go ahead with the appointment.

Edith drove Claire south on Route 101. They took a South San Francisco exit leading toward the bay, where the land was parceled out to light industry and science labs. Following a route that wound past the lawns of an industrial park, they came to a red brick building with a simple sign: Limb Dynamics, 56 Athena Way. While Edith waited in the car, Claire went through the glass door, where a man with warm eyes grasped her hand

"Dr. Hurd tells us you're a weaver," he said. "It will be a pleasure to work with you. We've got a simple device which can do surprising things. Come with me. I want you to meet our specialist, Carson Suzuki."

He led her into a large room where a slight, gray-haired man bent over a work table, polishing an object that reflected the light. Above him, in a glass case, a Japanese samurai sword gleamed.

Carson Suzuki himself was working with the help of an artificial left hand that moved gracefully in tandem with his physical hand, as he showed Claire what he had been polishing and said a similar device could be hers.

She warmed to the clean look of the device.

"It's clasp, not claw." She fingered the artificial hand's sculpted curves. "Beautiful."

"Yes, looks are more than skin deep when it comes to a proper tool."

Dog, Mallard, and Raven watched at the back of the room and I joined them, feeling uneasy about the samurai sword. "What's the point of displaying a weapon like that in a place making artificial limbs?" Was

97

this some grotesque joke?

"Tools that do not look alike or even act alike may be similar in quality," Dog said. "In the right hands, the sword is pure Bu."

"Boo?"

"Bu," he repeated. "Budo. The way of stopping the spear." An image appeared of a warrior moving at the speed of lightning to prevent an opponent's strike.

"And this hand he's making for Claire?"

"It too will move precisely."

I saw the connection: the silvery hand shone with accuracy, as did the double-edged sword hanging above us. But was such exactness appropriate for Claire? Dog sent me an image of a long-haired fellow dressed in animal skins slowly chipping a glistening black rock to a fine edge, not letting his eyes move away from the rock.

All right: a lineage of skill has been passed down from ancient times. Still, I wondered about the old fellow with those blooming biceps and the rock he was turning into something lethal, sharper than anything you need for trimming the knots of a rug. This powerful claw-hook-crescent-moon-hand Claire is getting--is it wiser than it needs to be, crafted with a thousand years of martial alertness?

Today Claire returned to Limb Dynamics, where the silver hand was fitted snugly into place at the end of her right arm, now prepared to receive it. When she moved her shoulder, lightly or strongly, forward or back, the claw opened or closed, and she could pick up a bottle, an umbrella, a pen, even pieces of string. The lost fingers ached as the silver hand entered their territory.

Here at home she shrugs and twitches the muscles of her back as the silver hand grasps skillet handles, lifts tea kettles, opens drawers. The hand was drawn to the excellent set of knives in our kitchen, engraved with those German twins. At first the silver hand wielded the knives with relish to slice the tomatoes and radishes for a salad. But our knives were overdue for sharpening, and the hand lost interest.

Claire often pauses to reflect on the swaying branches and fog outside the kitchen window, or the way the sun strikes the Oakland hills across the bay. She lets the impression fill the moment. But the silver hand doesn't operate that way. Picking up a utility mug, Claire looked away for a moment, and the mug fell out of the silver hand's grip and shattered on the kitchen floor. When she reached down to pick up the pieces with her other hand, a sharp edge sliced into her thumb.

The mug had been rather ugly, machine-stamped with misaligned daisies. I remembered how Carson Suzuki had spoken about the silver hand's pedigree of beauty. What if something didn't have a pedigree? Was it possible that the hand disdained to handle the mug?

With the silver hand, Claire applied a bandage to the cut and sat at the loom to weave. She picked up a length of russet yarn, and for the first time the hands worked together to pull the ends of the wool through to the front of the weaving into a Persian knot. And another and another.

When the lost hand refused to share her pleasure, she went back to the mirror box, practicing the looping of the yarn, the deft pull-through around the vertical threads, hoping the phantom hand would agree to the mirrored movement. But it still ached.

What did it want, anyway?

Dog appeared and motioned me to a bare wall in the basement we were eternally finishing. A brush and a can of paint were offered, and I covered the entire wall with incredible sunset hues. I pressed a small sponge into the bright ground, whereupon an opening appeared that held the image of a lion's head— eyes, nose, haunting eyes of the huntress. With shimmering gold paint, I traced the outline of her head, holding the sable brush with attention and care. I pressed the sponge in another place, and a new image appeared—a man's strong face with eyes that spoke of what was Real. Other images bloomed out of the vivid ground--a fir tree, a turquoise lake, a rose—and as they appeared I stroked their contours with golden light.

I said to Dog, "These colors . . . there's nothing like this on earth, is there? I had to die to see these colors, didn't I?"

He lifted a paw and waved it toward the glowing images of the sunset painting, and a veil covered them so that they looked dull and ordinary, toned down and darkened.

"That's not the way they really are," I said. "Can't you change them back?"

But he left the colors that way, as if to say I'd need

another painting lesson.

When I came upstairs, Claire had relaxed the threads of the loom, put away the yarn and gone to bed. She'd left lighted the lamp by my desk, and it shone on a photograph of us taken once upon a summer time, in a boat at the lake.

CHAPTER 17: THE ESTATE

ON BOTH SIDES of the gate a wall built of stones fitted together without mortar stretched into dense woods. Rick walked downhill along the wall until he came to where the hillside dropped off into a nearly vertical ravine thick with brambles and loose rocks.

He returned to the gate and followed the wall in the other direction. The wall ended at an oak tree which stood at the edge of a steep descent. He made his way past the oak, thorns catching at his pants and shirt, then moved down the brambly slope, tangling and disentangling himself until he came to the road which the truck had taken.

Somewhere a rhythmic pounding sounded—slow, not quite regular, gathering force for the next blow. The sound grew louder as Rick approached, and then the next blow did not come, as if a listening had begun. Rick stepped into a clearing, where an old man, tall, erect, and muscular, turned to meet him, a sledge-hammer in his hand. Nearby, a series of posts stood firm at the edge of a stream, each post a little higher or lower than its neighbor. Gangly tree branches rested atop the posts and angled out over the water.

"What are you doing here?" The man stood with his legs spread and anchored, eyes sparking under the brim of his canvas hat.

"I heard the sound. My ride let me off, and I could use a place to stay tonight."

"I don't let strangers on my property. I don't want you here."

Rick recalled how no one entered the Adams estate, with its three hundred acres of forest and pasture and rivers, without permission. Once, years ago, he had seen Walt Adams buying saddles at the livery place in town, saying little, accepting the respect of the shop owner.

"I used to live around here, when I was growing up," Rick said. He didn't expect it to make a difference.

"Just leave. People don't come here unless they're invited, and no one invited you," the old man said. Rick recalled stories about the old man and the ways he had of refusing, of testing.

"Get out. However you came in, get out."

Rick retraced his path up the hillside, through the brambles to the long stone wall that ended at the oak. It was dark now and he bedded down not far from the tree.

It was cold on the hill in December, and Rick lay awake for a while, telling himself that the old man had the right to give orders, but that his no might not be final. Eventually he fell asleep, and I settled in to watching, as starlight filtered between the oak's branches and fell on Rick's face. Later, as he tossed and cried out in his sleep, I wondered if it might be possible to generate a bubble around him that would keep off the bad stuff. But he kept churning and calling out, and I let the bubble idea go, content that the starlight fell on his face, and that a circle of radiance fell on him that took me in, too.

Suddenly, sharp claws broke open the material I have now. Eyes an inch away stared at me, and a fierce beak tore at my substance, then vanished. Had I been too slow for something, not recognized some omen? What had I forgotten? Swallowed whole without question? Or hadn't caught on to?

Here I was, following Rick and Claire around, shuttling between the two of them, always being told I was forgetting something. Old resentments beckoned. But I was unwilling to visit them and told myself to let them be.

It came to me that we were all part of some Experiment--something intended in a way I didn't understand. Maybe I could be content to be part of this unknown effort, about which the Animals perhaps knew only a little more than I did — an experiment including them and me and Claire and Rick, all of us bound together by blood, water, and, perhaps, Spirit. An experiment that might succeed or fail.

Even so, I itched to know what was going on.

The next morning Rick went down the hillside again, following the dirt road. Gradually there were sounds, a hammer tapping, a rooster crowing, and the back of a big house, with a door opening into a kitchen and the smell of coffee. Rick lifted a garbage-can lid and saw orange peels, half an apple, banana skins, edges of toast, egg shells. He reached down for the apple and the biggest piece of toast, but before he could touch them a hand weighed on his shoulder and he turned to face the old man. "I told you not to come back," the old man said. "Get out."

"Could I have something to eat?" He spoke directly, as the old man had, looking him in the eye.

"Jean, give this fellow some breakfast. Then see that he leaves. I don't want him here."

A straight-backed, lean woman in jeans and a colorful floral blouse appeared. "What's he doing here?" she asked.

The old man ignored the question and said, "Jim Hagerty's here with deliveries. Make sure this fellow's in Jim's truck when he goes back to town this morning." He turned away and walked around the corner of the kitchen and out of sight.

Jean, who had an unexpected softness around the mouth, led Rick into the kitchen and fed him the breakfast he had seen fragmented in the garbage can: two soft cooked eggs, toast spread with jam, a mug of coffee. "Are you the fellow Mr. Adams spoke about last night, the one he kicked out?"

Rick nodded, and she said, "Can't take a hint?"

"I guess not, ma'am. I hoped I might be some use here."

"You know this country, do you?"

"Yes, ma'am. Since I was a kid."

She told him to wait for the truck. He sat out near a barn full of tractors and neatly hung tools. Beyond the barn another building held shelves of dried fruits, home-canned vegetables in Mason jars, and uncombed hanks of wool in shades of beige, off-white, and dark brown.

Jim Hagerty appeared with his pick-up truck and ushered Rick into it while the woman Jean watched. She would tell the old man he had left.

Hagerty angled the truck out onto the gravel road. "Got kicked out, did you? It's not the first time that's happened." After a while he talked about how he knew the old man's family. They had been conventional ranchers for generations, living off the land and not treating it unreasonably, as most people viewed things.

As a young man, the old man had seemed in the same mold as his father and brothers. But when he came back from the Viet Nam war, years after it ended, after spending time in India and Japan, he sold off the cattle and worked to bring the land back to where it was before cows over-grazed the pastures and messed up the streambeds. His experiments with farming and animal husbandry were not radical or showy, Jim Hagerty said. But small things added up, and the land was now restored close to what it had once been. People on the outside didn't know much about what happened on the estate and the old man didn't care about spreading the news. His path differed from his father's, but it was a path that was good for the land. And it seemed good, too, for young people who heard about it and came there.

"If they can get in." Hagerty gave Rick an understanding nod.

Back in town, Rick caught a ride with a farmer heading in the direction of the estate. The man let him off a few miles from the turn-off to the estate, and Rick didn't try to catch a ride again, thinking people might begin to recognize him. When he came to the road leading up to the gate, he didn't expect anything would be different, that he'd have to hike around to the end of the wall, make his way down the ravine and follow the stream to the main house.

To his surprise, the gate was unlocked, and the way lay open on the road that wound through the woods. He walked in and followed the road, listening to the sound of the stream below and to bird calls, nearly muted in the cold season. A squirrel peered at him. Below him were the posts the old man had been pounding, and now he recognized their purpose: long heavy branches from the trees along the stream bank were propped up on the posts, sometimes with a flat stone to ease the fit between the branch and post. A tree limb which otherwise might break off had been allowed its full length and shaded a bench or an Adirondack chair. Farther along the bank he noticed a smooth, trapezoidal stone which appealed to him. He picked it up and took it

107

along with him, thinking it might fit in somewhere.

He heard the thump and whir of machinery, chickens cackling, voices calling. A muscular yellow dog ran out and growled at him, then held its ground, barking but not attacking. He stopped beside a boulder marking the edge of the woods and carefully balanced the trapezoidal rock on top of the boulder.

Then the old man was walking toward him, quieting the dog, saying, "All right, you're here. You might not like it, though."

Which was how Rick came to the estate.

The Animals seemed fond of the place and mysteriously familiar with it. They immediately settled onto the platform of a dilapidated tree house up in a big oak tree at the edge of the meadow, and I joined them.

"How come?" I wanted to know. "What made the old man change his mind about Rick?"

Dog turned it around for me. "What made Claire decide to call Sylvia? Or, for that matter, what made her decide to marry you?"

"Or stay married?" Mallard whispered.

"She saw beyond appearances, I guess." My looks hadn't been outstanding--I was on the thin and bony side, while Claire was and is beautiful. I was grateful that she'd seen beneath an inauspicious exterior. In the same way, perhaps, she'd listened to something in Sylvia's voice in the phone message.

"Maybe Walt Adams saw something in Rick," I said. "Still, he's an ornery type, and he and Rick might trip each other up."

"Stones are for stumbling," Raven croaked.

"And for marking the way," said Dog.

CHAPTER 18: WHEELS

"I WANT to buy a car," Claire told the support group. "The insurance company has sent a check."

"Way to go," Don said. "What are you looking for?"

"Something sturdy, and it doesn't have to be new."

Francie said, "Well, aren't you the sweetheart, pushing yourself to get back up to speed."

Jeff opened his mouth. "I'll help you find a car."

"He knows about engines," Edith said.

"Ron Murphy Pre-Used vehicles." Bright triangular flags flapped in the breeze at the used car lot, where a variety of late models stood in rows. The little group — Claire, Edith, Don, and Jeff — strolled almost to the end of the first row when a salesman spied them.

"A well-built car up to five years old? No problem at all. What about this nice little Stadium sedan, four years old, low mileage, great shape?"

"I'm here with my mechanic. When I see something I like, he'll check it out." Jeff nodded, with a seriously enjoying look.

For two hours, Hank the salesman produced keys for one car after another, which Don, with Claire and Edith as passengers, drove around the block, then out onto the highway and back. Jeff's injury didn't get in the way of sliding underneath one car after another, after which he shook his head and said a word or two: "bad brakes" or "suspension" or "muffler."

"Say, are you folks in some kind of recuperation unit?" the salesman asked.

They arrived at a medium-sized compact, a hybrid in a well-polished shade of turquoise. "Good engine," came from Jeff. Thirty thousand miles over five years: the car was barely broken in. The salesman took Claire for a ride, while Don rode in the back seat and thought it had decent shock absorbers and would be a good ride for Ashford. The salesman said it would be delivered to Claire the next day.

Full of excited talk, they drove back to Edith's, with Jeff grinning silently in the back seat. "This will be a good car," Claire said. "I'll practice driving in the neighborhood."

Late the next day the car was delivered. Sitting in the driver's seat in the silent garage, Claire trembled at the thought of starting the engine, backing the car out, and venturing into the street. The bucket seat hollowed itself out and she fell into the darkness of the accident again, the phantom pain rehearsing its agony.

111

The memory of my darkening body returned, and I felt less than useless. I withdrew to the kitchen and waited there until Claire came up from the garage into the kitchen, poured a glass of wine and began to make dinner, lighting half a dozen candles against the dark. Wine wouldn't work for me anymore, but I was with my dear wife, sitting with her at the table, watching her lift her wine glass. The atmosphere glowed. The car could wait.

Judy came over the next day, not pushing at all, and she and Claire sat together in the garage until Claire's breathing calmed down. The silver hand pressed the starter button, and the car started. The hand popped the shift lever into reverse and the car backed out of the garage. Useful habits reappeared, the silver hand's movements coordinating with what Claire's body remembered. They proceeded down the Excelsior hill toward Mission Street and the cars that honked when Claire hesitated as traffic lights turned green. I hovered in the back, hyper-watchful, as we re-traced part of our final route.

Don came along on Claire's first out-of-town excursion, a trip which took them up through organic dairy farms and Miwok sites to the headlands of Point Reyes. Her driving steadied itself, the two hands working together. On the way back to San Francisco, as they rounded the blind bend of a hillside, a cow started across the road. Claire hit the brake barely in time, freaked-out horror rising in her, the phantom hand screaming its dismay.

While they waited for the herd of Jerseys to pass, Don, like a superior officer at a debriefing, listened while Claire gave a report on the experience. It was a good thing, he said, to know you could be afraid and still handle the situation. On the way back, they stopped for a beer, and he drove the rest of the way.

Charley brought over an unwashed sock of Rick's, and Claire put it in the back seat of the car next to Ashford's blanket. A few days later, Claire and Edith, with Ashford in the back, drove north, up the coast toward Mendocino. At a highway rest stop, Ashford insisted on showing her where, halfway up a hill, two pines framed a flat-topped boulder with a good view of the parking lot and the passing traffic. Bushes screened the boulder, and someone might have watched from there without being seen.

Off and on, the Animals rode along with us, and Dog took a shine to the little mutt. "He's serious," Dog said. "Keeps an eye on what counts."

"Like his next meal. *Quawwwkkk.*"

Claire's driving was more than satisfactory, even though the phantom hand complained bitterly as the new hand took over.

"Something is wrong," I said to the animals. "Nothing helps the pain in the missing hand. What's going on?"

"What have you observed?" Dog asked.

I came up with something that took on authenticity as I spoke. "What's left of her arm, nerve endings and tied-off muscles and blood vessels and such, seems to be

113

grieving for what's lost, the and that was destroyed in the accident."

"And is that all? The alive grieving the dead? Wishing for the beloved flesh? *Necrophilia*?" Raven inquired.

I felt my way toward something else. "Maybe the arm is mourning a part of itself which is still alive. Something that is lost."

"And where is it?" Mallard gave me a wistful mallard-mother look. "Where did it go?"

I plunged into fairytale thinking, which made more sense than anything else. "Maybe the accident scared it off and it has gone into hiding."

"*Quarrkkk*. Hide--and seek."

The next week Claire and Francie drove south, to Hollister and the Pinnacles. While Claire and Ashford walked among the volcanic extrusions, Francie took a shorter stroll. When they met back at the car, Francie said, "Claire, this is a lovely place. But the compass needle isn't pointing in this direction." To Claire, too, it seemed an empty exercise, and she didn't head south again.

Judy called, sounding apologetic. She and Greg had both been so busy they hadn't done anything about hiring a detective. That was still a priority, she assured Claire.

"Things take a while to work out," Claire said, thinking that Rick might need all the time available.

"Mom, if we wait for things to 'work out,' we'll be sitting here next year."

114

Claire changed the subject. Arguing with Judy might move hiring an investigator to the top of the list, and that could disturb the workings of whatever a benign providence had in store for Rick.

"How are things at Home Safe?"

Judy's job--stressful, demanding, important--took up the rest of the conversation. But Claire knew that Judy was checking on Rick's case every week, and the moment would arrive when she would go beyond inquiry.

I echoed Claire's phrase when I met with the Animals. "Rick can do himself some good at the estate. But he's going to need time to work things out."

Raven yawned. "What mortal doesn't entwine himself in the need for more time? But to work things out?" He examined the phrase gingerly, holding it at wingtip. "What does that mean?"

Mallard, the capable paddler, said, "He keeps moving, anyway. That's a plus."

"And then there's moving like a tree, in tree time," Dog said, and I glimpsed the rhythm of branches, swaying as the sun flickered through summer leaves.

Thumbing through an issue of *The California Crafter*, Claire found a notice about a weaving workshop in the northern part of the state, up toward Mount Shasta, "specializing in traditional Near Eastern designs." Claire copied down the information and sent off an email inquiring about the workshop.

A woman named Jean Harmon wrote back: yes, they

studied tribal weaving and made both knotted rugs and flat-weaves. She wrote, "We weave rugs developed from traditional designs, following the ways of those old weavers as much as we can, improvising as they did." The workshop was ongoing; Claire was welcome to join it whenever she arrived. Weaving with one hand, or with a prosthesis? It was up to her; Jean Harmon didn't see why not.

A breeze came in through an open window, a crow ruffled his feathers on the telephone wires, and Ashford trotted up, wanting a walk, his harness in his mouth. Once outside, he turned away from McLaren Park, and started north in the direction of the Golden Gate Bridge, eight miles past the corner of our street.

That puzzled Claire, but when she woke the next morning, a bell was ringing, hard, inside her. Yes, she'd go. The lost hand would come with her, part of the baggage, along with the silver hand and its precision. *And,* I whispered, *our blood too, Rick's and mine, compass-pointing north.*

"You're planning to drive this car *where*?" Judy said. "To Humboldt County? In the winter, when you might run into any kind of weather? And if they catch Rick Mendoza, you'll have to come right back."

Well, of course she would, Claire said.

She called Sylvia to tell her she was leaving on a trip and would keep in touch. Charley came on the phone. "I'll bring you something when I come back," she told him. "What would you like?" He'd want Rick, she realized with a pang.

But Charley surprised her. "Can you bring me back a rock? Rick and I are starting a rock garden."

Edith called to postpone the support group meeting. Jeff was having one of his "spells," a word implying he wasn't in the crazy shape taking him to the doctor meant.

Claire realized she was leaving the members of the group as they were, engaged in the struggles that had supported her own efforts and that would change in unknown ways before she returned.

CHAPTER 19: GABIONS

AT THE ESTATE I have been blending and watching, trying for the kind of observation the Animals encourage. As a skeptic, I avoid hasty judgments and opinions picked up from passing influences. Still, even without a physical body I am stuck with these blind spots--of wanting, insisting, judging, envying, "fixing" — and I can only hope they won't completely blot out my glimpses of the View. This investigation keeps on and on with no solution, only the occasional insight. I'm trying to stay with it.

The Animals themselves now prefer to use an imagery which, like the trees' language, is impossible to translate adequately. Speaking crudely, an image of the light passing through quartz crystal might translate as Accept your Transparency. A mallard chick frightened at its reflection in a puddle: Things are not what they seem. A dog nosing and pawing fragrant roots: *Watch. Listen. Dig.*

But often there are neither words nor images, only long silences that leave me exposed.

"I feel naked," I complained to Mallard. She lip-synched an approving quack and lifted out of the water, spreading her wings against sky and the wide angle of the mountain. It was all very well for her, I thought, a duck who can take off and find something new any time she wants to, while I'm weighed down with assumptions I'm not even aware of.

Which can be discouraging, unless you're lucky enough to have Mallard fly back to you and whisper, "Lovely, my dear. To sense the weight. Lovely."

Rick kept quiet as much as possible around the old man. If he opened his mouth in front of Walt Adams's probing gaze he wouldn't be able to lie, and he wanted to hang on to whatever security the estate offered.

Jean put him in an upper room under the eaves. The room held two cots, one of them made up for him, and one empty. The window near his cot viewed the bare boughs of walnut trees. The first night he slept for a while, woke shouting out of a nightmare, then slept again till morning.

"Walt wants to see you right away," Jean told him after breakfast. "You'll need these." She handed him a pair of rubber boots. She didn't say where to wait for the old man, so Rick carried the boots down to the stream and stood under the long propped branches that reached

119

out over the water.

"We need more of these." The old man stood downstream, half-camouflaged in mottled shade. He pointed toward a neat wall of stones lining the steep stream bank. Rick looked more closely at the wall and saw a network of steel wire, crisscrossing the bank at four-inch intervals, which held the rocks in place. In some spots ivy crept along the network and concealed the wire.

Nearby, a wire cage with an open lid stood empty. Farther downstream were more cages. "Gabions," the old man announced. "Your job will be to set them into the bank, fill them up, wire them shut. We need fifty feet of gabions, all the way down this side of the stream. It stops the erosion."

The old man told Rick to find stones in the stream bed of the right size, not too big. Rick remembered how, up at the outpost, they fortified a hillside with rocks and wire and concrete. When he mentioned this, the old man shook his head. "This is different. You're way off base if you think it's the same." To Rick it didn't seem so different.

After Walt Adams left, Rick put on the boots Jean had given him and paced along the stream, which seemed full of stones the right size. Quickly he scooped up enough to half-fill a gabion. He hunted in the stream for more stones, his hands cold but lively as he picked up smooth stones, blue and black and grayish green.

He ate the lunch the women packed and went back to work. By mid-afternoon, as the sun slipped over the

120

edge of the ravine, he had filled four gabions with scooped-up rocks and secured them with a twist of heavy wire. And he had prepared the bank by digging back into the clay soil so that the first gabions could be fitted in. There was a long way to go, but he had made a start.

The old man stood above him on the bank. "What do you think you're doing with those stones?" he growled. "Picking them right out of the stream where it's convenient for you, is that it? Leaving holes that can change the course of the stream?"

Rick stared at the old man.

"Dump all those stones out and put them back where you found them," the old man said. "From now on, don't ever take two rocks from the same place in the stream." He strode off.

Rick flushed with anger. He opened one of the gabions, grabbed a rock and hurled it into the stream. He threw another, then told himself he couldn't afford to argue with the old man, any more than he could argue with the sergeant back at the outpost.

He returned the next morning and undid the work of the previous day, emptying the four gabions and returning the stones to likely places in the stream bed. After that he set about finding rocks which didn't know each other well.

He trudged upstream with a burlap bag, picking up stones, never more than a couple in any location, putting them in the bag. After the bag was heavy and half full, he slid its stones into an empty gabion, repeating the operation until the gabion was filled and firmly settled into the bank. One was filled and tamped, then two. Sunlight spotted him with warmth as he worked under the trees.

"You dumb fool, what the hell are you doing here?"

Rick stared at the old man. "You told me to start here."

"Can't you see this isn't the right place?" Walt Adams said. "Start farther down the stream and work on this section later, if you want the bank to hold. This part comes later, as any idiot can see." He stalked away.

"You mean here?" Rick called after him, pointing to the spot he thought the old man meant. No answer from the old man's departing back.

"Son of a bitch," Rick said. The old man paused a fraction of a second in his departure and inquired of the trees, "Now how did he know my name?" Above the stream, crow laughter.

Rick couldn't figure out what was wrong with where he had placed the gabions, and he decided to leave them in the bank. When it made better sense, he would take them out and find them another place. He moved down stream to the spot the old man had pointed out, where exposed roots dangled above eroded clay, and went to work with a shovel, gathering stones from a widening area.

After a while he lost whatever understanding he had of why he was standing in the slow-moving stream. The bank's slippery verticality discouraged the thrust and scrape of the shovel, and the ragged voices of crows were in mocking syncopation with the shovel's blows. Rick's shoulders ached, and acids of fatigue spread through him.

He remembered the old man saying, "You dumb fool," feeling the odd benediction in Walt Adams's resonant voice, a warmth operating beneath the surface of insult. He returned to the gabions, carefully piling stones into the wire boxes, twisting the lids into place. For a time, as the light dimmed, the work seemed to go by itself.

The crows were closer now; two of them conversed softly in a pine tree just down the creek from where he worked. "*R-r-ruk. Quuark.*"

As Rick returned to the main quarters in the deepening twilight, the women were preparing dinner in the kitchen. Through a window above the kitchen he glimpsed an upper room, warmly lighted. Inside the room, two women stood in silhouette on either side of a weaving, moving it around to find the right place on the wall to hang it. The colors were vivid, the design bold and angular. Walt Adams came in the room and stood watching while they fastened the weaving in place. Rick remembered glimpses seen through binoculars at the outpost: flame-like thrusts of a design, gold against indigo, on a loom in the open doorway at the house of the beautiful woman.

After Rick was asleep, I met with the Animals in the moonlight outside his room. A newcomer appeared at the edge of the clearing, a disheveled-looking cypress with the massive, fluted trunk of the ancient cypresses in

123

McLaren Park. Like those trees in drought years, it reached out scraggly lower branches while the needles in its upper branches stayed dense and dark. Behind the tree stood a boulder of lordly presence, like one of those massive rocks in a Zen garden surrounded by the smaller stones it protects. Or like the rocks ringing the pond at McLaren with their long-continued presence.

Mallard, Dog, and Raven shared images with me: Rick fingering the gun, Rick screaming inside his nightmare, but also Rick present to the touch of the rocks and the softened light through the fir branches, images implying that the estate was having a good influence. Rick could still be dangerous to himself and to Claire, I told them. But the Animals insisted that the perils of our mingled blood challenged us in a good way. There was a science in watching, Dog let me know, and there were special instruments for seeing.

"You're ahead of me there," I told him. "As an investigator, I think I know how to weigh the data and keep on questioning. Is that what you mean?"

Dog sent me the image of a sea captain's long viewing scope, its antique leather surround and golden fittings bathed in an intense light, an instrument able to reveal facts that were also feelings. At which surmise the image obligingly took the shape of a magnificent burnished cello sounding deep angelic tones.

The image faded. Dog remained in front of me, his gaze taking in all of me—the outer scene all the way to the tatters, and then the inner scene, all the way to the part that was still Mason.

Looking at the ragged cypress, I wondered how it regarded its own life, threatened by neglect and drought and burrowing insects. I knew it was just trying to survive, like so many fragile creatures of our planet. No use feeling sorry for it. After all, it was alive, and in a place where it gave shade and seeds and perches and routes for scampering. And oxygen itself.

Dog said, "Now you can take in more of the View. You've begun the Bowing."

"The bowing?"

"The way you just bowed to the Cypress." He meant something about respect, I think. Which must be a lot like realizing that someone is actually *alive*.

"Look up," Dog said. "See them?" He pointed toward the top branch of the Cypress. I rose with him to where we peered into a nest of sleeping hawks, downy half-grown infants among them, their adolescent feathers sprouting, their heads tucked into their wings. One of the infants rustled in his sleep, and I saw how his hues of pale beige, tan, reddish brown, tawny orange were shaping, feather by feather, into a striking pattern. He would be a beautiful bird.

"Go below the feathers," Dog said.

"Bow to the inside, not the outside, dear," Mallard said. I remembered what I had understood moments before about the life of the Cypress, and I waited for Raven to remind me I'd forgotten. But he only gave me a long serious gaze.

"There's the Bowing," Mallard said. "And the

125

Entering." She beamed optimistically.

"The Entering? It's too soon for that," Dog said.

I returned to the room above the walnut trees where Rick was sleeping. Around midnight someone tiptoed in, laid down a duffle bag, dug around in it to find and light a flashlight, undressed, and climbed into the other bed.

Rick's nightmare took him to the hilltop in Afghanistan, where boulders came hurling toward him. He saw his friend torn apart and woke to his own yells. In the dark, a hand shook his shoulder: "Easy, guy." A table lamp clicked on, and a young man with stubby pale hair was leaning over him.

"You don't want to stay in that one," the newcomer said.

Still half in his nightmare, Rick struck out against the hand.

"Lay off. I'm all right."

He lurched away from the touch and made his muscles go taut. The mattress rustled as the other man settled back into bed. After a while they both slept, and when Rick woke the next morning, the other bed was empty.

As the old man woke and rose before the winter dawn, the backward pull toward sleep reminded him of his wish to move upstream against the ceaseless flow of daily life. The young people who came to the estate wanted that, too, and I thought of the salmon who climb the stones of a descending river as if they were steps on a stairway.

The old man dressed and went down to the kitchen. Ravens, big fellows, flapped down to peck at scraps. Lucy came running up to greet him, nuzzling him, her heavy body bouncing against his. Jean, who was making lists and watching the simmering oatmeal, looked up at him, risking his gaze. He looked back, taking his own risk.

The Animals were drawn to the quiet times early in the morning when people sat motionless on cushions in the barn. I liked to be there, too, as the space filled with silence. The Animals gave me to understand that This Side and the Other Side often came together here, and the Thread linking me and Claire and Rick pulsed calmly as I experimented with bowing to the people who came in to sit.

Rick came late to breakfast and squeezed into the one chair remaining, which was next to one of the women I'd seen in the upstairs room. He glimpsed her abundant long dark hair, shapely nose, olive skin. It was tight quarters at the end of the bench; his arm touched hers as he reached for the coffee pot, and he sensed her quick withdrawal from the contact. Which caused him to be shy about turning his head past the coffee pot. When the toast basket came along, and he reached it toward her, she took a piece of toast with a quiet half-nod, as if to let him know that he wasn't what she had withdrawn from. Rick was about to ask if she wanted the butter, when the old man's penetrating voice filled the room. Was Jean satisfied with the wool for the carding and spinning? Some of it seemed coarse to him.

"We're willing to deal with what's there," she said. "Of course, nobody objects to fine wool, especially the workshop people at the Bridge."

"Then check the back of the barn before you go."

The workshop people, the Bridge — Rick remembered the building he had seen spanning the creek, outside the estate, on a deeply rural but public road. Who came there?

Next to him the beautiful woman sprinkled salt on her egg with slender fingers, lifted eggs onto fork, raised fork to mouth. Exclamation point for curve of lip and cheek.

"I know who she is," I told the Animals as we waited down by the stream after breakfast. "Maria Warp." Maria's picture had been all over the internet for a few days after her child's abduction, and again when the little girl's body was found. Now, on the estate, Maria is out of the public eye.

"Which means," I said to the Animals, "that there are two people who need to stay hidden here. The whole situation just got more complicated, didn't it?" At which Dog sent me an image of Walking, one step at a time.

After breakfast Rick went down to the stream. He soon had enough rocks for another gabion and began piling them into the cage he had settled into the bank.

"What the hell do you think you're doing?" The old man stood above him, his face a mask of anger.

That bastard. An iron ball rose in Rick's chest,

128

pressing against his breastbone.

"Unbelievable," the old man said. "What sort of stupid ass are you, working here by yourself?"

In Afghanistan, there had been a sergeant who expressed similar astonished disapproval.

"Maybe that's a good question?" Rick drawled.

"We *never* work by ourselves here," the old man said. "I'm sending someone to work with you and I don't want you to move till he gets here. Who knows what god-awful mistake you'd make?" He disappeared up the bank.

Rick sat down and watched a leaf whirl into the stream and a small daisy open its shaggy bud. He felt the feathery itch of his back muscles, the ache of tendons seeking movement, the tightness in his chest. Above him on the bank two crows sauntered stiff-legged, uttering what sounded like *"Woak!"* or maybe *"Work!"* Rick allowed the crows' voices and the faint rustle of branches to settle in behind the muscles of his belly.

He heard footsteps on the gravel path by the stream. Maybe the old man was sending one of the crew who came and went from outside on weekends. They were young and good at what Jean called "maintenance," a catch-all term covering anything that needed attention-- drains, roofs, floorboards, sheet metal, clotheslines, tractors, trees. See-do stuff. He had seen one of them weigh an ax in the palm of his hand, getting acquainted with it before he used it.

"Hi, how are you doing?" Rick recognized the voice that woke him the night before. "I'm Dave Jackson." A young man with a stub of pale hair and a relaxed, bear-like body reached out and shook Rick's hand.

"I don't know why the old man has you working here by yourself. These gabions are definitely a team thing."

Dave Jackson picked up a burlap bag, handed it to Rick, and set off downstream at a rapid stride, motioning for Rick to follow. He selected a stone and held it inquiringly to the light, then his arm circled down toward the burlap bag in Rick's hands. As the stone fell into the bag, Dave Jackson was already moving on, looking for the next stone.

"Did the old man tell you how particular he is about picking stones?" he asked Rick. "He doesn't want to disturb the places the stones have found for themselves, or the stream has found for them. Makes sense, after a while."

Dave Jackson tacked from one side of the stream to the other, spotting-picking-lifting stones from the stream bed. He swerved, took long steps or quick small ones, went now on this side of the stream for a stone and then back to the other side, boulder-hopped across and back and across again, always ready to send another stone into Rick's bag. It was not a small thing for Rick to be available for the next stone.

The bag got heavy, but Dave Jackson kept going while Rick dragged it over the rocks of the stream bed. Briefly the bag got stuck on a protruding rock, came unstuck and bumped onward over the stones, got stuck again. When the bag snagged on a rock or fallen branch,

Dave Jackson adjusted his own motion so the stone he was holding was ready to drop into Rick's bag just as the bag came unstuck. And, for a while, their watching and moving and bending went smoothly.

When the bag was nearly full, they brought it upstream to where an empty gabion waited and set it down next to the gabion. Time for a break, Rick figured.

But Dave Jackson said, "Next step?" Scooping up a handful of stones, he held them above the open gabion.

Rick suddenly was fed up with all this alert bullshit, this going forward without stop; now, he supposed, it would be about alertly dumping rocks into the gabion. He'd had it with this guy, who was like the old man, always pushing. Who had spotted him as a screamer the night before.

Dave Jackson let go of the stones he was holding and they clattered harshly into the open gabion. Rick tensed; it was the kind of noise which told the enemy where you were. "Idiot," Rick said, keeping his voice low the way they always did at the outpost. "You could mess it up for everyone."

"Sorry. Giving away the position with a stupid move."

Rick relaxed, and grinned. "Afghanistan?"

"Iraq." Dave Jackson said that he'd been in the Kirkuk area and seen months of action before being wounded and discharged. When he returned home he hadn't been able to pull it together, and there had been an assault charge. After working through an anger management program in Redding, he found work on the

Adams estate. At some point, he said, he stopped scheduling his own death within the next 24 hours.

Rick nodded. "Wanting to get out of everybody's way."

"Yeah, then you can be lonely forever."

"What kept you from that?"

"Realizing I wanted to take other people along with me. Scary."

I did take someone. Rick remembered he was "Robert" at the estate and let Dave Jackson's words settle without response. Then he said, "It's about family, too." It frightened him to think how Charley or Sylvia or his mother would react if he killed himself.

"Having buddies helps, too," Dave Jackson said.

"Most people don't know anything about buddies."

Dave Jackson nodded. "Unless they've been there." He began sorting through the rocks spilled into the gabion, checking on their place in the wire cage and how their shapes fitted with the rocks beside them. Most of the rocks settled in, having already accepted the move. But sometimes he noticed a sharp-edged refusal and returned the rock to the stream bed.

Rick watched him for a while, then joined the sorting.

CHAPTER 20: IN WHICH LIMITS ARE EXPLORED

WHEN WE MET in the woods beyond the sheep pasture, the Animals seemed remote and tentative, while I was full of eager reports. "The bowing helps," I told them. Every time I bowed, a sudden shift took place from the Outside to the Inside of myself. When I'm chattering to myself about a bird's feathers or an off-putting facial expression or someone's fussy quacking, I'll remember about the Bowing, which takes me inside and changes everything.

The Animals listened, then went silent, which usually indicates Something Else, not always pleasant. They went off and huddled in a circle bathed in a soft light, where it looked as if they were speaking not only to each other but to some invisible Presence.

Left with the Cypress and the Rock, I realized I had forgotten to bow to them. So I bowed and was startled at the grave acknowledgment of the Cypress that rose from its roots, like the upward slide of *Rhapsody in Blue*. When I bowed to the Rock, its veins deepened into rose, and some neighborly lichen took on a creamy glow.

The Animals returned from their huddle, and Dog said, "We've agreed on the next thing, in Consultation. You may practice Entering now."

"Though it's *very* early," Raven muttered.

"There's an urgency," Dog said.

"I'm not sure what you mean by Entering," I said.

Mallard said, "It's simple, dear. Entering is Joining, and it can happen with any being at all--a star, another planet, an animal, a plant, a rock, a person. One lives inside and shares their life, every bit of it. Without interfering, of course."

"To *inhabit* them?" I recalled my disastrous attempts to take over Claire's left hand and the horror of those moments frozen to the piano.

"Not *that* kind of inhabiting," Dog said. "To truly Enter and Join is entirely different, as you're aware from the Bowing." Entering another creature, he let me know, is a kind of service and should be treated as such.

"I hope we're not talking about shape-shifting," I said. Shape-shifting, if that was what he meant, sounded like the left-handed black magic I often found investigating paranormal claims. But the animals dismissed my concerns. "Call it shape-shifting if you want to," Mallard said. "We call it Entering, and it is highly respected on This Side, dear. It's another step toward becoming useful."

134

"What about the tatters?" A few muddy shreds are still hanging off me. "I can't even get through a wall."

"You haven't been noticing, have you?" Mallard inquired. "Try." And now my hand passed lightly through the trunk of a young bay tree, and then through a nearby redwood.

"All right," I said. "That's the good news. But passing through something or someone is different from going inside and staying for a while." That felt scary.

"There are constraints," Dog said. "You may experiment only with animals and plants. No human beings." All right, I had a history of getting stuck in the human body.

"You can consider me off limits, too." Raven settled his feathers. All right. Human entry, and Raven entry, was off limits

"Now you must prepare," Dog said.

The Animals put me into a dream-like state that took me inside one creature after another. I was in the golden lean body of the dog I'd run over. He was whole, and we ran happily, paws hitting the ground, ears slicked back in the wind. Then I entered the goldfish that expired on the dining room floor. I flicked my golden tail and knew her life. Then I found myself inside the poor rabbit I'd once watched being frightened to death. In the Animals' experiment, I entered him and hopped in the grass and nibbled at lettuce and listened well with my long ears.

In that dream-state I went in and out of each creature freely and smoothly. Boundaries were nonexistent, and my dream-self moved into dog and rabbit and fish and came back out again at the call of Raven or Dog or Mallard.

"You're showing me Disneyland," I said. "The tame stuff I was brought up with. Is that realistic? And what about all those animals who aren't tame at all?" I thought of totems I hadn't been given—like wolf and bear and eagle.

"We're dealing with what's here for you, dear, and you might as well, too." Mallard spoke more briskly than usual. "The Entering isn't all bliss, but there *is* joy in it."

Raven grumbled, "*They* think you're usable, so you might as well think so too. *Quawwwwkkkk.*"

So I accepted what they'd shown me of my experiences with those animals, with certain things emphasized and others omitted that perhaps were just as important. Something in me relaxed and accepted that. That I might be of use was a thought that filled me with unexpected delight.

CHAPTER 21: CANDACE

I AM in a new place, a park-like landscape heightened to exquisite beauty. The animals are nowhere to be seen, though I feel they aren't far away. It's peaceful here beyond anything I've known--the stream bank covered with vigorous ivy, no need for gabions; magnificent flowers of rose- or dahlia-caliber, a river sparkling over rocks, fish swimming in sinuous rhythms just below the surface. Rapturous birdsong, colors glowing from each plant or fish or flower and blending into the neighboring glows.

I pride myself on being keen-eyed, able to pick up small details. As a kid I idolized Sherlock Holmes, who could take in the tiniest fact and fit it into a rational explanation, and I had wanted to be like him. Here the details were clear and vivid, but without explanations. I know of no technology capable of recording those colors and lights, yet some faculty I have access to takes them in, here in a new place that is definitely on This Side.

Someone approached, singing in a sweet piping voice.

"O yearning of the tree to be

Its newest bud

O yearning of the heart

To send its freshest blood" —

It was about time. This Side must be heavily populated, but I had seen no one except for my guides. And now, someone was singing.

"Grandpa, I'm here!"

She came to me, in those moments before her next Awakening. Candace, my granddaughter, not yet born.

She was no infant, but a girl of eight or nine, standing under the trees in a costume from the far reaches of the Amu Darya or Turkestan—full rippling indigo skirt banded with mosaics of embroidery, a blouse with a bride's load of beads and intricate stitching, soft white leather boots, flowing scarves, the bangles and beads that tradition--and eight-year-old girls--delight in. Her brown waist-length hair flowed from the hairline's V above the heart of her face.

Music rose from the ground below us and the branches above us, laced through with morning sun: the thrum of balalaika, the deeper iambs of a tambour. And she danced, softly at first, then wildly as a flute intervened. I danced too, swooping her up into the leafing pear tree where a hummingbird's throat glinted red.

There were many dances to learn, or perhaps remember. She caught the flavor of rhythms and sent them to me. And my substance found ways to step quick or slow, to leap into unfamiliar movements that she already knew. Even the hummingbird's evanescent flight showed her fresh ways to move.

"You'll be a dancer," I said.

"Isn't everybody a dancer, Grandpa?"

"Well, you'll be one, darling girl."

She laughed and we danced some more. She taught me a song or two, and I found my own words--lullabies, mostly of the Leonard Cohen sort--fitting themselves into a music we could share. I had never practiced singing, but now my voice felt full and rich.

Then, like a change of weather, the music heaped itself into the clashing of stones and howling winds. And Candace cried out that it was Time.

No, not yet, not supposed to be. "Stay with me," I sang to her, the words finding musical urgency.

But she cried out, "They say it's Time to be born . . ." and the winds gathered her up.

"All right. Don't forget me."

"I'll be back," she said. "I promise. I'll come back to see you."

"Promise me you'll come." I heard Raven's objecting groan.

"I promise." Then she vanished.

Pain shot through the filament — the pain of Claire, who was going to be a grandmother, unless I messed things up.

139

The Animals were on my case.

"All right, Candace is your granddaughter," Raven said. "But a promise is a problem. You haven't learned that yet, or you wouldn't yell 'Promise me you'll come.' *Quwarrkeueu*."

I wanted to protest that Candace herself said she wanted to return and I had simply affirmed it. But I didn't argue with them.

"Your daughter Judy likes to get things done, doesn't she?" Mallard remarked. "She'll be going into labor any time now." The last time I saw Judy she was not pregnant, and certainly not ready to give birth. But time here is slippery, bendable, spitting out short and long segments like coins of varying value. I had a grandchild who'd be going to the Other Side any time now. I wanted to see her again in the worst way, despite what the Animals said.

Claire, Candace. A harmonious combination. Claire would grieve if anything happened to the child we'd both hoped for. Wishing to have Candace back, wishing for her to stay, was I asking for something sinister without realizing it? Maybe a long line of consequences, reaching far into the future?

The image shifted, and I was looking at a red-haired baby, her hands reaching toward the golden birds of the mobile above her crib: Judy, a few months old. And, half seen, my father's face, looking toward us, and fading away. Judy's grandfather.

CHAPTER 22: IN WHICH LIMITS ARE SEVERELY TESTED

RICK WAS PLEASED with what he had accomplished since the old man put him to work on the gabions: rocks harvested from the stream and piled up on the bank, wire baskets filled with stones and sealed with galvanized wire. Now they were fitting the second layer of gabions into the side of the creek. As he picked up stones from the stream bed, the newfound teamwork with Dave Jackson kept him confident — and careful.

"You asshole." The old man stood beside him, staring down at the creek bed. "What the hell do you think you're doing?" He pointed to the most recent gabions, placed where Rick and Dave had strategized about putting them. Where it made sense.

"Do I have to do it for you?" Before Rick could say anything, the old man tore loose the topmost gabion with his bare hands, wrenched open the cage's lid and dumped the stones at the water's edge. He pointed downstream. "I want them there. And these too!" He reached toward another gabion.

Rick reddened with anger as the rocks spilled into the stream. As I threw out images to remind him of all he stood to lose, he rushed at Walt Adams and grabbed for his throat. "You goddam f---ing son of a bitch!"

A flash of movement, and the old man stood several feet away from Rick, well out of reach, and Rick was grabbing at empty space.

"For Christ's sake, when are you going to use whatever brain you've got?" Standing in midstream, the old man spoke without haste. "Get back to work." He climbed onto the bank and strode off.

For a moment it was silent. Then two crows watching from above the stream, resumed their comments: "*Woak. Woak. Woak.*"

Is that all, Rick wondered. He had been ready to choke the old man with his impossible demands. The old man his benefactor. Why hadn't Walt Adams kicked him out for good?

Dave Jackson came up. He had been downstream and had seen what happened. "Man, you looked like you were ready to kill him."

"I know. It scares the hell out of me. The old man--"

142

Rick broke off. "I told myself I wouldn't let this happen. And he just walked away."

"Yeah. He won't let you do what he goads you to do. He's incredibly fast."

They went back to the cool rocks, the scattered gabions, making simple moves that cleared the atmosphere. Rick was shaking, and I felt something humble in him, like the prayer for altitude of a pilot trying to pull out of a spin. The filament linking him to Claire and, indirectly, to me, gradually calmed.

Later, Rick walked the stream bed alone, searching for stones, running his hands over each stone's contours and picking the ones which seemed to offer themselves. In mid-afternoon he returned to the kitchen, where Jean sent him with another load for the compost heap. Out in the meadow Dave Jackson and three of the other men were doing strange leaps and whirls that resembled the old man's way of moving. Repeatedly they moved toward each other, offering strikes that were received with quick turns, joins, and redirections which sent the attacker into a backward fall or a forward roll.

As the twilight deepened, the old man showed up, and Rick watched while the younger men came striking toward him. Just as their determined fists and blade-like hands should have reached him, they were striking into the empty center of a circle which Walt Adams stood well outside of.

They each took a turn with the old man, and with some small movement he confounded their intent and stayed unavailable to whatever they tried, twisting or

143

turning to send them tumbling by their own momentum into falls and rolls. Then he walked off, taking in Rick's presence at one end of the mat.

Back in their room, Rick said, "What was that? Can I try it?"

"When I first came here, I wanted to do it too. It's such great stuff, something he learned in Japan, after Viet Nam. But the old man said, 'What if I let you do this, and you feel threatened by somebody who's going a little too far, or you think he is? What if you lose it? What kind of situation would that put me in?' He wouldn't let me practice with anybody but him for the first six months."

"Maybe you'll show me a few moves?"

"Not yet." Dave Jackson turned away.

CHAPTER 23: AN ARRIVAL

IT TURNED OUT that Candace didn't go anywhere. Something must have been worked out. Birth on the Other Side could wait, and once again we were picnicking together, dancing, and singing. Had the perception of time been adjusted? Had pregnancy, with its slower rhythms, calmed Judy's eagerness for accomplishment? Had my plea for Candace to return made a difference?

I overheard the Animals discussing reconsideration from a higher Source. "They think she might still be useful here," Dog indicated. At least that's how I interpreted the little plum tree blossoming in space.

As Candace and I sat down for a game of "21" in a garden where splendid dandelions vied in their beauty with roses and orchids, a sheet of paper floated down beside me. I picked it up and read it, while Candace jostled against my substance, trying to read the message.

There was a familiar salutation, printed in the hand of the small writer of the earlier letter.

Dear God, its not scary like before I died because I'm with Mama. She says we're safe. But its lonely here. Please find us. Love, Elena."

"You know what 'died' means?" I asked Candace.

"Of course, Grandpa. I've done it lots of times. But what's the use of being alone when you're dead? Why shouldn't there be people around?" She worried about Elena, although on This Side a better word than "worry" needs to be found.

Then W. C. Fields showed up. And had no use for kids, dead or alive.

In the '30s of the last century W.C. was a popular film comedian, capitalizing on an Archie Bunker-like persona, morose and insular. Because they stole his scenes, he disliked children. He had been an early joiner of the Skeptics Society, and our oldest members passed on stories of his out-and-out denial of anything which couldn't be weighed and measured, and of his outspoken assertions about human stupidity and gullibility. He hadn't publicized his membership in our society--which may have been just as well.

Claire and I had watched a couple of his old movies, listening to his whiny, assertive, take-me-or-leave-me voice with its outrageous pronouncements. I'd sensed an odd dignity in him, a weird self-respect that went deeper than the surface of boozy self-satisfaction. Somehow you knew he suffered for the way he was, yet

146

had no intention of giving it up. It was up to you to bear it too and find the humor in it. He had been a take-charge kind of artist, sculpting his films to his own satisfaction--except for one movie, *David Copperfield*, in which he humbly enough followed direction in creating Dickens's character Mr. Micawber.

W. C. left the planet in the mid-1940s, and I was surprised to find him still in the beginning stages of the afterlife. I went over to his table, where he sipped a highball and scanned the action at the 36th hole, and introduced myself, with a reference to our mutual membership in the Skeptics. He ignored the introduction and eyed Candace.

"This golf course is for adults, not kids," he said. "What is she doing here?"

"We're getting acquainted while she waits to be born," I told him.

"What the hell does that mean?"

"My daughter's having a baby and she'll be it, when the time comes," I said. "I died rather suddenly, in an automobile accident, so I won't be around when she's born."

"What are you talking about?" He pinched up his face and wrinkled his honk of a nose.

I tried again, and didn't see how I could be clearer, but he stared at me and didn't bother to reply.

"You do understand that you're on This Side?"

"It looks like a decent place for a vacation. I had a bad case of flu, edging into pneumonia, and decided to take some time off and come here, take a few days to

147

recuperate."

So, the guy was not aware he was dead. "Traveling by yourself, are you?" I asked.

"I always travel by myself. My last girlfriend finally got the idea and gave up trying to come along. Other guys take their wives on trips--you know, for the maid service. I take just me and my camera. The homebodies can see the pictures when I come back if they want to."

"And your kids?"

"Kids? Don't have any. Well, hardly any." He shrugged, shaking off some unavoidable memory. "Not on your life, pal. If the ladies wanted to be with me they needed to settle for that. They always told me I took care of the kid issue all by myself." He chuckled. "The ones with a sense of humor, anyway. 'Who needs a kid when I've got you?'"

Candace was listening to our exchange and looking baffled. Not that she was entirely clear about things, but this guy was coming from a whole other direction. "Is he a grandpa, too?" she wondered.

"More like an uncle. You could call him that, if you want. You aren't likely to run into anyone quite like this guy."

Candace picked up her little frame drum, stroked its center lightly and thumped deeper around the edges, half dancing already. She twirled and a skirt with a vivid satin lining flared around her, a Carmen sort of skirt. She went up to W.C. and made an offer: "Will you dance, sir or uncle?"

He looked at her as if she had suggested that he take

148

off his socks and walk across burning coals. "Take it someplace else, kid."

"But dancing is the most fun!"

"I'll dance the day bananas turn blue." A line of blue bananas stretched out like a picket fence from the stream below up to where he was sitting.

He turned to me in disgust. "Do I have to swear at her?"

"She likes to dance and thinks you might like to as well," I said.

"Forget it, kid. *Fahgeddit*. I try not to move except to pick up whatever I need," he said, reaching over for the drink he could always find.

Candace got me on my feet then. On This Side, I can pass for a lot younger than 52, more like 30. And dancing is amazing here. You bounce up high, practically sprout wings, land on a daisy or a rose bud or brush a swan's wing. The rhythms change often and you're there for the change, bright and intense.

W. C. watched us curiously, then decided he was seeing whatever he usually saw and went back to his whisky sour.

"Why won't he dance, Grandpa?" Candace was puzzled.

"He doesn't know how."

"I'll teach him!"

"That's a great idea, Candace. He'll get the hang of it by watching us."

Mallard the Dancing Duck arrived, briefly amazing W.C. with the timing and power of her short legs. But

149

soon he returned to his usual expression of sour disbelief.

"What is W.C. doing here?" I demanded of the Animals. "How can someone be here without knowing he has died?"

"He knows things are different," Mallard said. "But they don't fit his definition of being dead."

So he didn't, or couldn't, see straight. His hearing didn't seem good either; his ears filtered out the music Candace and I heard.

Candace snuggled on my lap, her wavy brown hair brushing against my substance. Three glowing balls appeared and W.C. juggled them flawlessly, something he was good at in his early movies. Seeing that was encouraging, for a good juggler can't be hopeless. And Candace was delighted.

He put away the balls and groused, "When is the kid leaving? Do we have to hang around here till she gets born?"

"I hang around because I want to. You don't have to." He got up and ambled down the path toward another lounge where he could set up an acceptable scene with a bottle of bourbon and no surprises.

Chapter 24: New Directions

"HOW DOES the old man know how far he can push Rick? Or does he?" I wondered to my advisers as we met down by the creek on the estate. Mallard stepped off the rock where she was perched and scouted in the stream bed until she found a stone with a long flat side. She lifted it to the bank with her beak, then vigorously rubbed her beak against it. The friction sent up sparks, and she gave me a slanting glance. The right stone, the right beak?

In the following days, Rick watched Dave Jackson and a half dozen of the younger men and women practice the martial art. Most were beginners, and Rick repeated his request that Dave show him at least the first moves.

"It's still too soon. What if you're practicing with a woman and you imagine a problem, how are you going to handle it?"

Rick looked on as Dave showed the others how to meet, blend with and re-direct an attack--and how to fall, an essential of the art. They took falls easily enough, though Rick still wasn't sure why anyone would agree to fall.

When Dave Jackson instructed his partner to grab his wrist as hard as he could, Rick thought that finally there would be strong-arm stuff. But Dave moved with the grab and changed direction, and the other man found himself far out of his comfort zone, his stubborn grip stressing him toward a broken bone. "Let go, now," Dave commanded, and the beginner relaxed and took the fall that released him from danger.

"Take hold tightly, let go lightly," the mantra formed itself. Something about knowing the right moment. And did "tight" and "firm" mean the same thing? I observed their experiments and remembered clinging to my dying body, then hearing the urgent "Out of there!"

In the vision the Animals had arranged, I had entered other beings without resistance, and I approached the Rock and the Cypress with the thought of deeper acquaintance.

Just bow and go in, I told myself as I faced the dark Rock. Surely it was patient, with its long ripening, its million microscopic entrances. But it was also dense with a billion years' pressure, and my substance thickened in fear. I shied away. The rock was a potential prison. *Nothing doing.*

152

The Animals watch, allowing me to find my way. Letting my failures educate me.

I try to be with Rick as much as possible, hoping to send an encouraging sign or image. *You screwed up with the old man, but I'm not giving up on you.* In the room above the walnut trees, Rick reached into the drawer, took the revolver out and let it fall from palm to palm as he looked out the window toward the dark pines at the edge of the meadow. Wings flashed past, and a great blue heron flew into the nearest pine--a vision of elongated grace followed by utter stillness. *Look, Rick.* And Rick did look, the quiet of the heron entering him.

He tucked the gun in his jeans pocket and walked out into the twilight, to where the old man was standing above the creek, taking in the propped trees, a bird's evening call, dinner sounds from the kitchen. Now the old man silently waited for him.

Rick reached into his jeans pocket for the gun. He didn't want to keep it anymore. He'd give it to the old man.

Walt Adams stared at him, his questioning expression hard and unyielding.

Damn him, always challenging. Rick left the gun in his jeans, its bulge at his hip. Knew the old man saw it there. Walked away.

The next time I met Candace she was standing in front of an easel, wearing a smock that covered the sparkle of her bangles. She dipped a brush into jars of paints available in endless colors and began painting, working from a tiny white center on the thick vellum-like paper. Above the intense speck of white, she painted glowing spots of color, and a tower of lights---reds, golds, blues, greens, purple--rose above the brightness at the center of the vellum. Below and above the tower, stormy grays filled the scene, as if threatening its light.

"It's a picture of her, the one who sends us letters. Elena."

She took down the painting she'd made. Beneath it was a clean sheet of cold-pressed vellum with the creamy matte texture I remembered from the art supply store, where Claire bought sheets of it to sketch and paint designs for weaving.

Candace handed me a brush. "Paint, Grandpa."

This time a deep indigo settled across the sheet like warm night, thick and opulent, and I dipped and re-dipped the brush in a bottomless reservoir of midnight sky.

Galaxies appeared as points of light rising to the surface of the paint, one after another till the darkness lightened with a million Milky Ways. Still, the dark space between them held out its claim, and like a kid connecting the dots, I drew links between galaxies until a Being made of stars shone among drifting nebulae. Ravens and dogs and ducks flickered along the star-branches. Then the imaging ended, and the Unknown filled me as I stood beneath the tent of light.

"Grandpa, that's a nice picture," Candace said. "Though I like mine better."

On weekends, when more people came to the estate,

154

a few of the men peeled off from whatever they were doing to work with Dave and Rick, twisting wires or digging deeper into the creek bank to settle a gabion into place. They worked quickly, as if something was at risk.

"What's the rush?" Rick asked Garth, an older man who usually worked on carpentry projects. "You guys act like these gabions are a priority."

"The old man doesn't necessarily see it that way," Garth said. "He discounts the big flood we had a few years ago. Hundred-year stuff, he says. But the big ones have been coming more often, and we'd like to get something in place before flood season."

He said that Piper Creek, which ran through the estate, came down from the hills full of water from the snow pack higher up. A few years earlier the creek had filled far up its banks, and the Mendocino, the river which Piper Creek feeds into, flooded. Work on the gabions began after the flood year, for it was feared a bigger flood might carry away the creek banks and put buildings underwater. But drier years followed, and the work slowed. "The old man hasn't forgotten, but it's harder to feel the urgency."

The weaving studio built over the stream was precarious, Garth said. Walt Adams thought adding more gabions would take care of the problem. "But it might not be enough."

"What would be enough?"

"Hard to say. We'll try to put in a few more gabions than the old man has in mind. It'll make a difference."

The next time Garth came to the stream, Rick let him

155

know he was glad to consult about the gabions. And Garth stopped off whenever he was on the estate, even when it was late, at the end of a full day.

As leaves deepened into gold, Rick remembered how, in his family, so many things needed to get done for the holidays: so many flowers to coax into blooming at the right time, so many pine wreaths to wire together, so many ribbons to tie. Working with the gabions had a similar flavor. It had been more intense at the outpost, where the slightest mess-up could cost huge. It wasn't like that. But it wasn't entirely different, either.

One evening, up in their room, Dave Jackson said, "We ought to figure out this place better." On his next trip to town he googled a map of the watershed. Now they saw how Piper Creek and Sweetfalls Creek joined and made their way down to the big river. Tracing and marking maps, researching local geology, they widened their knowledge of the watershed.

"Here's where the workshop is," Dave Jackson said, pointing to a spot a mile or so from the main gate. "It's a pretty location, and fifty years ago somebody thought it was quaint to build the workshop across the stream. The construction was good enough, but over the years erosion has eaten at the banks."

Rick wanted to know what went on at the studio, and Dave filled him in. Jean and Maria handled the weaving, and occasionally visitors arrived for a few days, people who had found the workshop online or in some obscure magazine.

"The studio is a quarter of a mile off the main road

and not too close to the gate," he said. "Not hard to find, but not obvious either. Other than the weavers, the estate doesn't have much contact with the outside."

The next day they stood looking at the weaving studio, a covered-bridge-like structure stretching across the stream, its ends anchored in the opposing banks of Piper Creek. Exposed roots of bankside trees dangled in shadow beneath the studio.

"This is where we need to work," Dave said, "though the old man might not agree. I mentioned the situation to him a while back, but he just waved me off. He likes to keep our work away from the edges of the estate. Doesn't want publicity, or the chance of it."

"Then why does he bother with something as public as the weaving studio?"

"A visitor to the weaving studio doesn't have to be aware of the rest of the estate, so the old man puts up with it. Besides, Jean's a force in herself. She's interested in these tribal designs going back hundreds of years. She went to that part of the world years ago, before the place blew up, and figures she's preserving something in danger of being lost. The old man can relate to that."

When the Animals and I met that evening at the stream's edge, I pointed out the eroding banks beneath the Bridge studio. Looking at the December woods, Raven wanted to know what wasn't an eroding force, from one perspective or another. The fruitfulness of summer a mere preparation for winter's decay. And vice versa. Dog added images of mountains weathering into the volcanic sand of Pacific beaches, and that same sand pressed and folded and twisted into new mountains.

"*Quawwwwkkkkrrrkkk.*"

Raven stared at me, and I woke to the realization that I had lost touch with the thread. Its hum had slipped out of hearing as I became involved in the erosion question, and I had forgotten my connection to Claire and Rick. I returned to an awareness of the vibrating filament, relieved to be linked again to the vast and permeating View.

Raven glanced slyly in my direction. "'Vast and permeating?' *Quawww?*"

I got it: a glimpse of how the View soon enough turned into another proud segment of the Forgetting.

CHAPTER 25: CLAIRE'S JOURNEY

GREG STOPPED BY and helped Claire load the car, carrying Ashford's kibbles, harness, leash, and cushion down the stairs into the garage.

"I'm traveling light," Claire said. "I'll stay in nice places where they have beds and sheets and blankets. No need to rough it."

"Is your hand letting you alone?"

She shrugged. "There are twinges."

"Twinges are worth listening to."

The phantom hand ached, hard, as the silver hand skillfully unlocked the trunk of the car.

Early this morning Ashford settled in the back with Rick's sock, I took my place in the seat beside Claire, and we started out. Dog has downsized to fit into the car, and is getting acquainted with Ashford. He has taken a shine to the little mutt. "He's serious," Dog told me. "Keeps an eye on what counts."

"Like his next meal," I said. Dog nodded benignly.

Claire's driving is more than satisfactory, though there's pushback from the lost hand as the silver hand takes over. After lunch today she took two ibuprofens, which meant she was getting plenty of pushback.

Hours later, with night coming on, we still had miles to go on back roads. But Ashford slept comfortably in the back seat, and it felt cozy. The twilight deepened, and fat soft snowflakes plopped against the windshield. Claire switched on the headlights. Just ahead of the car a bird flew across the road, its tail flashing white.

The snow fell faster and the wipers swished across the windshield. Why weren't the headlights catching the snow in their beams? Claire flicked the lever to test the high beam.

No light. Nothing.

She braked the car, left the motor running, and went outside to inspect. Ashford reared up, questioning, then settled back into the warmth of his bed. Both headlights had gone dark. Only the parking lights on either side of the car displayed buttons of yellow light.

It was fifty miles back to the nearest gas station, twenty to the next one north. Cell phones didn't work deep in the country, and another driver might not come by for hours. She got back in the car and edged it forward. The snow had let up, and she could see the ditches on either side of the road. At moments, the wind sweeping across the pavement cleared off patches of

160

snow to reveal the white stripe running down the middle of the blacktop.

Stay warm, I told her. *Go slow.* You'll be all right if you can see the white line. There's extra gas in the trunk, remember?

Then came a shock of black, an abyss of darkness with all signs wiped out. After a frightening interval, the feeble return of the visible--the strip of paint, the hillock of brambly snow at the road's edge. Then darkness again and the tense search for a sign.

Tires scraped over gravel, and the car hovered at the edge of a ditch. Claire slammed on the brakes, swerved back on the blacktop, whipping the steering wheel in helpless violence that almost took the car off the road again.

She turned off the motor and waited in the darkness, nerves firing, the phantom hand throbbing.

Remember the flashlight?

Well, of course she did. She took it out of the glove compartment and switched it on. She considered rolling down the window, holding the flashlight trained on the middle stripe, and proceeding that way. But she needed to keep both hands on the steering wheel, and she settled for putting the flashlight on the dashboard, where it beamed out toward the road, catching the center stripe. She inched ahead at five miles an hour, which was too fast. Three, two miles an hour. Ashford was sitting up now, staring into the darkness ahead.

The car hit a bump and the flashlight rolled across the dashboard, careening onto the floorboard. Claire stopped the car, picked up the flashlight, and replaced it on the dashboard. She edged the car forward until it hit an unexpected bump that sent the light tumbling down again. She braked again.

Ashford chose the moment to scratch at the rear door. Claire retrieved the flashlight, fastened his leash, and let him out. She followed him along the side of the road. He was in no hurry, savoring the smells of a walk on a walk-less day. Suddenly he halted for an enticing scent and the leash went taut. Claire was pulled off balance and fell on a patch of ice that pitched her down the sloping bank of the ditch, the flashlight and the leash flying out of her hand.

Icy water splashed up over her boots and seeped into her socks as she inched her way toward the flashlight, which had caught on a stiffened weed two-thirds of the way down. She picked up the flashlight and threw it up onto the embankment, away from the edge, and scrambled up, her feet struggling for purchase, the silver hand grabbing at the frozen grass. She made it to the top of the bank and for a little while lay stretched out in the snow. The wind had stilled and I could hear her heart pounding and could sense the lost hand's protesting ache. Ashford was topside, peeing into a craggy weed, his leash dangling from his harness.

As Claire raised herself up from the snow, a light winked between the trees. It disappeared as she stood up, but by shifting her angle, she could keep it in view.

She got Ashford back in the car and started the engine. The flashlight hinted at what looked like a driveway, with rutted tire tracks in the snow. The car turned into the tracks, and the light she had seen from the ditch burst into alert sentinel mode. At the end of the driveway was a small frame house, lighted by the bulb, framed in darkness.

The car labored ahead a few more feet and shuddered to a stop, as a man and a woman came out of the house, their bodies backlit by the fierce bulb. They were young, the woman no more than thirty, the man a little older. Haloed in the spotlight, the woman's open, unlined face was warm with welcome. The man, darker and more guarded, stood a little behind her.

Claire explained her situation. "Come inside and get warm," the woman said. "It will be good for Garth and me to have visitors," she smiled, noticing Ashford. "You're welcome to stay with us."

"I'll check those headlights in the morning," the man said.

Claire was shaking hard. Tears came, and for a little while she couldn't stop crying.

"It's the blessed relief of meeting. We feel that ourselves, in the winter, when someone comes. It's so good to get out of the cold." The woman said her name was May.

They went into the warm house, and May seated Claire in an arm chair, where her shaking subsided, and there were warm socks to put on her feet and a braided rug for Ashford's bed. May brought Claire a hot drink, milk with a bolstering of brandy that went down in a calming way.

163

Claire offered to help May with the meal she was preparing. "Let yourself rest," May urged. But Claire followed her into the kitchen where May was adding a place setting at the broad-leaved table. "Give me something to do," she said. She held out the silver hand, smiling, asserting its competence, trying to ignore the throb of the phantom hand.

May handed her a wooden wand with a hook at its end, pointing to a trap door in the floor where there was a place for the hook to grab. When Claire inserted the hook, the door rose and hinged back to rest on the floor. Wooden steps and the shock of cold led her into a room carved out of the earth beneath the house. Hanging from the joists in the dimness was what she guessed to be a side of lamb. Stacked on shelves above the dirt floor were rounds of cheese and jars of butter. Mushrooms shouldered their way out of rich decay, and jars of seeds saved from a summer garden awaited another spring. Milk and cabbages and beets fermented in heavy crocks; mason jars of tomatoes, green beans and carrots stood near bins of turnips, parsnips, and apples.

Claire paused in the dimness, awed by what the root cellar represented. She fell into a dream of the earth, its color and richness, the cornucopia of nature spilling into the root cellar, guarding and offering its plenty to those who lived here.

She was roused by shooting pain in the phantom hand and saw that the silver hand had snatched up a score of parsnips and apples and was depositing whole cheeses into the basket she carried. Generosity, indeed.

164

"Let's put those back," she directed the hand, which obediently re-shelved most of the vegetables and three whole cheeses which she was sure May did not need for their meal. She returned into the kitchen carrying what she had been asked for, root vegetables and a single round of cheese, to May's inquiring glance. "Is everything all right?"

"It's fascinating down there," Claire said. While her hostess peeled the vegetables, Claire put the silver hand to work stirring the simmering pot of soup on the stove.

The sky had cleared. Through the kitchen window the moon shone halfway to full, and stars appeared above the darkened trees. Claire opened the door for a better view. Garth was standing under the trees, taking a moment to relax, his tasks over for the day. I remembered times when Claire and I looked up together while night came on. She remembered too, and her eyes filled with tears.

"Don't let out all the heat," May said. Claire closed the door and went back to the stove, fork-testing the carrots as they turned tender.

Garth came in and brought another chair to the table. May set out the soup pot, Claire brought the bread and cheese, and they sat down to eat. Ashford gnawed on a generous bone and settled into his small round bed, mouthing the sock he guarded and prized.

Claire thought she'd never tasted anything like that soup, except once when she was five and hungry and far from home, and there had been a hamburger of miraculous flavor. This soup had that same intensity.

165

The phantom hand had quieted a little. As I watched them eat together, I felt myself fed by the sense of shelter in that room.

Garth said his family had been sheep ranchers for a few generations. After a college and a stint at an engineering job, he'd returned to the land. By then he and May had met and married.

May's family had lived on the outskirts of a city in southern California; she'd been home-schooled. Phrases with rhythms from Bible and hymnbook colored her speech-- phrases like "the blessed strain of meeting."

"Winters are rugged here," she said. "But Garth already knew the life--and I've been here now for a few years." There was a touch of rigor in her voice, and it struck me that if she were to speak of the "blood of the lamb" it would carry rich and specific meaning. She passed the bread to Claire with a legato grace that reached Claire. Once their hands, hers and Garth's, touched the butter dish at the same moment. A kind of rainbow spread from that, and the phantom hand sent its ache along the Thread.

"You're going up to Schoonerville for a weaving class? Garth and I have friends there," May said.

"I wanted to get back to weaving after the accident that killed my husband," Claire said. "My arm is healed, and I'm learning what this can do." She held up the silver hand. "I'm going to a place called the Bridge Studio where they work with tribal designs."

"I'm familiar with the Bridge," May said. "It'll be a good place for you."

166

After they had eaten, Claire climbed up to the loft, made cozy by the fire that still smoldered in the hearth. There was a single bed, covered with a quilt with circular interlocking designs, a chest with oak leaves at the pulls, and a frame loom with a half-woven rug. Animal figures, flowers that opened into sunbursts, a skirted hourglass figure blazed forth from the weaving.

Claire took the silver hand out of its socket and put it on top of the chest, where it lay metallically alert. She climbed into bed, the phantom hand rehearsed its loss one more time, and she slept.

Below the window, Claire's car sat quietly beneath the layer of wind-borne clouds speeding past the trees. A silhouette flew through the moonlit clouds, and Raven dropped into one of the cedars behind the house. He peered at the front tires, gave a satisfied mutter, and flapped off into the night.

Claire woke in a clouded dawn, the lost hand crying out, her body aching at the prospect of pushing the car north through the tunnel of wooded landscape. Dressing in the cold was a struggle, and when she came into the kitchen, May looked at her and motioned her into a chair at the table. "Caught up with you, has it?"

Ashford paced at Claire's feet, wanting to go out, to be fed. "Stay where you are," May said. "I'll look after him." Garth came in from feeding the animals, and May brought oatmeal and eggs. Claire ate a few bites before her stomach called a halt, the missing hand crying needily.

Garth said, "I'll look at your car now. The problem

might be in the wiring. I doubt that both headlights would burn out at once."

"One way or the other, I'll be able to go on," Claire said. But the thought dismayed her.

Garth offered bread to May, and again the current of a shared life passed between them. A closed circuit, Claire thought. They were moving through the day within each other's awareness, and she was going to be alone again. The phantom hand throbbed.

Garth went out to the car and soon returned, saying, "You've a gash in one of the front tires. And the spare looks like it was made for another car." He would order a tire that would fit, but he'd have to go into town to pick it up, something he hadn't been planning to do for a few days.

May said, "You shouldn't be going on today anyway. Stay here. We'll be driving that way in a few days, and we can caravan."

Garth nodded. "You'll have a tire by then."

"And you can work at weaving here," May said. "I have wool to card and spin." She placed a hand on Claire's forehead. "You've got a fever, do you know that?"

CHAPTER 26: SHIFTING SHAPES

MY EXPERIMENTS continued, this time with the Cypress. It had larger openings than the Rock and could be entered through a crevice in its rugged bark. But I thought of what waited for me inside the tree: insects to bite and dig and scratch at my shreds of physicality, knots and arthritic joints to trap me. Once again, I was afraid and held back from the Entering.

Had my instant death, merciful in its way, left me without a decent dying? It struck me that people who spend their last hours on a proper deathbed are better prepared than I had been for letting their bodies go and emerging reasonably transparent on the Other Side. I was still semi-opaque, unable to allow the Entering, even though some of the tatters had dropped off and I could pass through a door.

"Stop it." Cawing and flapping, Raven looked down

from a branch partway up the trunk of the Cypress. "Stop pushing." He quieted down, but kept to his perch.

I let my substance lean against the bark that flowed down the ancient trunk like braided rivulets of a stream. The untended branches, snagged and broken off, barely firred at their tips, didn't matter: Cypress was a mighty being and sheltered me. Why should I want to go inside? We already were related.

Close by the cypress, a few eucalyptus trees grew, their trunks shaggy near the ground, then slick and peeled higher up, the surface patched in warm cream and pale red. Raven took to sliding down those upper branches like a kid on a banister, modeling an experimental approach. He invited me to try it, and we slid down together accompanied by his squawky laughter.

Then the Thread lighted up with pain and yearning, and recess was over.

I like to hang out at the center of things on the estate—the main house where the old man lives, with the big kitchen on the ground floor and nearby storage and tool sheds. A muscular yellow watchdog named Lucy makes her headquarters near the kitchen. She has decided I am acceptable, and I arrive and depart without upsetting her.

Rick is only moderately capable of concealing his attraction to Maria. I liked to watch her, too, savoring her beauty as it sounds its overtones in me, remembering moments with Claire, when my body, even as it trembled with earthly desire, opened to another beauty.

Maria helps serve the meals, bringing the plates out from the serving table, and setting each plate before the eaters with grace and care. When she lowers Rick's plate in front of him, he tries not to let on how the move affects him. Something about the way she brings his food slows down his eating. I think it's because she is paying attention to him. *Let's have that in slow motion.*

Dog said, "She includes him but she's not playing favorites.."

"Goodness, no," said Mallard. "Maybe never." I thought of how her abuser had drawn a possessive circle around her. She'd broken out of Arnold Warp's prison and would want to stay out of anything that resembled it.

I pondered my own situation. Claire was not playing favorites either, with my blood and Rick Mendoza's mingling in her body. The tatters complained about that situation. A few of them, long enough to trip on and easily agitated, still hung off me. "They're dangerous," Raven muttered, and I remembered how Claire had sickened from my revulsion toward Rick.

But Dog gave me a kindly look. *Guard them.* An image appeared of a back yard like ours in the Excelsior, full of fennel, often regarded as a weed but also contained, watched over and treasured for its seeds and its unmistakable fragrance.

Are the tatters a needed reminder that I'm still not dead enough to accept them? Or, that I'm still not alive enough?

171

I try to include Maria in my watching. Often, when one of the men comes into her space, she looks frightened and moves away. I see the same shy, scared-off look when she looks at Rick.

"Nest marauders. *Quawwwkkk.*"

What is the pace of healing for such a wounding? The pace of water smoothing stone? Of young trees struggling to grow in a ravaged gully? Of birdsong returning to exploded hillsides?

"He didn't give Walt Adams the gun," I said to Dog. That hadn't changed.

"He knows he disappointed the old man. He needs to live with that."

I caught a glimpse of my father. At the end of one of our brief reunions, he was sitting at his desk in the office of the little resort in Michigan. "It was good to see you, son," he said, looking down, businesslike, as he opened a ledger. Then he looked up, his face open and lonely. I turned away and went down the path to my car.

CHAPTER 27: "YOU LOOK FAMILIAR"

I DON'T UNDERSTAND why the Animals are so tolerant of W. C. Aren't there limits? To get here, shouldn't there be a longing for something more?

Still, I have been on This Side long enough to realize that drawing conclusions is a fool's game. So I haven't asked the Animals about W.C., not after the first time. I'll find out what I can.

W.C. can be kind, if you aren't a kid or a cute animal. I've noticed how well he treats this person I think of as Minimal Man, a pallid, unobtrusive creature with a long, lined face and gray wisps of hair, He is gratifyingly unlike W. C., but is a *there* there? Passive is an understatement. He leans against a rock as if he needed the rock to prop him up.

When W.C. saw this guy, he went over to him, saying "Hi, Buddy, how ya doing?" in the softest voice. And sat down beside him, lifted the highball he'd ordered, offered it to him and watched the old guy switch it to orange juice and drink it with considerable pleasure.

They struck up a conversation, and it turned out they both loved old Hedy Lamarr movies. Back in the 1930's and 40's, Hedy was the Elizabeth Taylor of her day, touted as the world's most beautiful woman. She made films with the leading men of the time--stars like Clark Gable and Charles Boyer.

"But something outlasted all her beauty," Minimal Man said, "She was a great inventor. I still look her up every so often."

"You *know* her?" W. C. asked.

Oh yes. Minimal Man had been somewhere in the film business, one of those assistants to the second assistant director, the sort of thing which makes you a good living in Hollywood, though he spent his last years in poverty. He was on the set once when Hedy was filming, and they got acquainted. He found out she was co-inventor of an anti-jamming system for radio communication in World War II which in its developed form is still part of Bluetooth devices. "She was brilliant," he said.

W. C. said he had met Hedy a few times at Hollywood parties, and she struck him as a seriously intelligent woman, along with having all that beauty. "We used to discuss juggling. She was interested in the physics of it."

Had W. C. really been friendly with Hedy? It was the last thing I'd have thought of. But he has this odd respect for her, and she may have seen through his Scrooge mask to something she found sympathetic.

"Seen her lately?" he asked Minimal Man, shy hope in his voice.

"She's around. Shall we try to run into her?" They set off together, looking for one of those coincidences which are the norm here.

Dave Jackson spoke with Jean about the erosion below the weaving shed. She told him she would look into it. A day or two later I saw her talking with the old man and heard him say, "Well, have him come see me."

Later, after Walt Adams waded in the stream under the weaving shed with Dave Jackson, the old man said, "All right, a small crew then. No commotion up near the main road. But all right, start work, and stay out of the women's way."

The work on gabions was transferred to the stream under the weaving shed, where the occasional hum of a car or big rig in the distance competed with the voice of the creek. Dave and Rick worked there most days, with Garth and a few others helping on weekends. Which made not such a small crew.

Fraternizing was hard to avoid when weavers and the workers below them took a break at the same time

175

and the weavers knew that the workers were chilled in the deepening winter. On those days, the women served coffee and tea, fruit and cheese, in the studio. On warmer days, the women came out with apple or carrot juice, and the two groups sat together under the trees. Not exactly what the old man had in mind—the quiet conversation of Maria and Rick and Dave Jackson, with Jean too coming out to stretch a bit before the women picked up the pitcher and glasses and headed back into the weaving workshop.

I liked to follow them into the studio and view their work with its reminders of the Caucasus and Turkey and Iran and Afghanistan--knotted rugs and flat-weaves in vivid herbal colors. Pondering the designs, you had to wonder about the natural world surrounding those old weavers--did those flame-like hooks represent horned animal heads, or birds with necks curving down into water?

The Animals liked the atmosphere of the weaving studio, and we held our meetings at one end of it, near a weaving on which chevrons grew and reversed themselves. What was so compelling about these designs? I wondered. Dog put his paws together at the angle of a woven chevron in a gesture of prayer and longing.

An alarm went off inside me, and I beamed back to the estate. It was breakfast time on the weekend, a time when unfamiliar people often appeared. Down near the end of the table, Rick tried to make himself invisible. Weekends were risky.

A big man, heavy-jawed and sharp-eyed, sat at one end of the table, glancing around. "Brad Pointer," came Raven's hoarse whisper in my ear..

Pointer stared at Rick. "You look familiar. Raised in these parts, or did I see your picture somewhere? Did you always have a beard?" I felt Rick stiffening, not knowing what to say.

The old man's voice cut in. "Curiosity is the darnedest thing," he said, drawing it out, not unfriendly. "Around here we try to turn it toward ourselves, and a sure sign that's not happening is when you're poking around in other people's situations. Wouldn't that waste your time here?"

Brad Pointer fell silent. He'd keep those sharp eyes, though.

Struggling with an urge to run, Rick got up from the table and bussed his dishes, cup, and plate rattling against each other. He didn't notice Maria's glance of concern.

Later that day, Jean spoke with the old man while the others were washing dishes and setting up cushions for an activity in the barn.

"I could use him here," she was saying, not begging. I wondered if she guessed what had gone down between Rick and the old man at the gabions. Maybe she just knew Walt Adams well.

The old man said, "All right. Kitchen, garden, maybe dog." Jean nodded, good, was about to head back into the kitchen. "Part time," he added. "Those gabions still need work." She nodded. *Deal.*

"Is that a good idea?" I asked the Animals. Working closer to the main road, Rick would be even more vulnerable to sightings by people like Brad Pointer. "That guy Pointer could cause trouble."

"Pointer has a good nose," Dog said, looking at the bigger picture. .

The next morning, Jean said to Rick. "You'll be working here this morning. Take these out to the compost pile." Rick took the eggshells and orange rinds from breakfast and put them on the top of the compost heap, which surprised him with its warmth.

Back in the kitchen, Jean set him to peeling and chopping a dozen onions until his eyes watered above the white cubes. "Save the skins," Jean told him. "We make dye out of them." Then carrots and broccoli needed to be peeled and chopped.

One of the women, pert in designer jeans, eyed him speculatively and told him to cut butter into flour for biscuits to be served at the morning break. She would do the kneading and rolling. Later she directed him to a pile of walnuts to be chopped fine but not too fine. He chopped walnuts until Dave Jackson appeared, and they went out to find Lucy.

She was at the estate, Dave told Rick, because of the wild pigs living uphill. By the time the old man came back from his travels and started working on the place, those pigs had been busy for a while, tearing up the earth and trampling crops, even messing up the reeds in the pond. They could do an astounding amount of damage in a short time. Yet they were invisible, for they foraged at night. The old man went out and found Lucy, a young dog with a yellow coat and massive jaw--a Rhodesian Ridgeback, a breed whose ancestors had hunted lions in Africa. From the moment Lucy arrived, the pig problem was over. She roamed the place by night, circling behind the cabins, barking in her sharp baritone warnings up the mountain. The pigs stayed uphill and the gardens thrived. A Lucy had guarded the property for three generations of dogs, and the current Lucy had grown old.

As Dave Jackson brought Lucy's food in her steel dish, she rose from her morning nap, wagging her tail. Dave handed Rick the dish. "Here, you feed her. She's not hard to make friends with, if you're bringing food." Soon Rick was guaranteed a vigorous welcome, Lucy's body shaking with anticipation, aware of his presence even before he rounded the corner of the tool shed and she leaned her warm weight against him.

"The exchange of scents goes both ways, though with that feeble nose of his he may not realize it," Dog remarked at our next meeting.

"There's always food involved," Raven said. "Lucy knows who feeds her."

"There's food and Food," said Mallard, with a sharp glance at Raven. "Some people steal their food from other people's nests."

"Eternal vigilance. The lesson is right there," Raven said, with a beady stare in my direction.

I didn't see how his remarks about food applied to me. The food on this side is delicious. A few bites of coconut froth soup or a cloud-perfect omelet leave me completely satisfied. And I don't have to watch my weight.

"*Grawwekkk..* You've adjusted to the cuisine here. It's not that."

"It's that you're still in danger of being eaten up, dear," Mallard said.

I didn't get it.

"Going one way on a two-way street. *Quarrrkkkk.*"

"Eat and be eaten, dear."

"And what am *I* supposed to eat?" I knew she wasn't talking about coconut soup.

"Eat your fears," Raven said.

"Gulp down your anger," Dog added. "Or crunch it up."

"But then it'll be inside me," I said. "Isn't that a problem?"

"Digestion can happen."

"And who is supposed to eat me?" But now there were only images that I couldn't translate. Warmth and terrifying vastness, the covering tent of the sky ripped open. *Take it all in.*

CHAPTER 28: THE LIVES OF ANIMALS

CLAIRE CALLED JUDY and explained the situation. "I'm staying here for a few days. I need the rest. They're very kind here."

Things were easing up at Home Safe, Judy said. She would have time to work at finding Rick Mendoza. She could even come up to be with Claire. Would that be a good idea?

"It's beautiful here, and peaceful. Could things stay quiet a little longer?"

Judy said she'd talk things over with Greg. But there was an urgency they couldn't ignore as long as Rick Mendoza was missing.

Lucy began coming into Rick and Dave's room early in the morning, waiting for Rick to feed her. If he was having a nightmare, she woke him. At first, he was irritated at being disturbed, then realized she warned off the dreams the way she warned off the pigs.

Dog remarked that with a good watchdog things go better. I don't have a problem with that; hanging out with Lucy is relaxing. Rick thinks so too, especially when Maria brings the dog a special tidbit and there's an interlude of hanging out.

When Rick first arrived, Lucy silently patrolled the property in the night, occasionally sending a stern bark up the mountain. But now she filled the darkness with her barking. "It's her job," Dave Jackson said, "to be guarding the place with that genius nose." He continued studying the map of the watershed.

The barking pounded at Rick's brain until rage crowded out everything else. He grabbed the revolver from where he had stashed it under the mattress. "I'm going to kill the f------- dog!" he shouted and ran out into the night, as Dave Jackson stared after him.

It was cloudy and dark and quiet; Lucy had gone silent. Rick edged his way around the building and along the trees at the foot of the hill, calling her name. He heard her trotting toward him, and he cocked the gun. Once, up at the outpost, they had shot a dog that barked too much.

Then Lucy was beside him, nuzzling him, her body pressing hard against him. The darkness inside Rick fell away, and the feel of the weapon in his hand chilled him. Dave Jackson was there, his flashlight turned on Rick, its light shining on Rick's hands: the one that held the gun and the other hand hugging Lucy as she leaned against him.

182

They brought Lucy back into their room, and Dave Jackson instructed her to lie down by the door. She sat down reluctantly, and got up every few minutes to pace the room, her nails clicking on the floorboards. Toward morning, Dave got out of bed and let Lucy out.

Later, when Rick came outside, Dave was standing just off the path, pointing out the muddy hoof-prints and torn-up grass at the edge of the garden. He said, "The pigs knew when Lucy wasn't out there."

Outside the kitchen, Lucy waited for her breakfast, a long bruise on her shoulder. When Rick reached toward her to examine the bruise, she pulled away with a snarl. I caught a glimpse of her reddened gum line and wondered if Rick would see it. And then Rick did see, and Lucy let him ease her mouth open for a better look at the inflamed molar.

After breakfast, Rick and Dave drove Lucy to the vet in town, who anesthetized her and took out an abscessed tooth. Later Lucy rode dopily back to the estate and had a long nap. In the evening, she patrolled the estate silently.

"Good work with Lucy," Mallard remarked.

"I didn't do anything," I said. "Rick saw the tooth."

"You let the watching doing the work," she said. The air brightened as the new moon edged past a cloud.

Which was the moment when Rick took the gun out of his pocket and handed it to the old man.

"Community protection—is that what you have in mind?" Walt Adams asked, the gun resting in his open palm.

183

Rick nodded, still feeling the shock of the narrow escape with Lucy, the burning foreknowledge of remorse. He wanted to stay with that, even if it meant going all the way back into himself. I wished it for him, aware of the denial that was still strong in me, along with friendlier feelings.

The next day Dave Jackson handed Rick a white jacket and pants and a white belt, saying he could begin to train. In the days that followed, they practiced martial arts attacks and responses on a mat under the big oak outside the kitchen.

In the few words he spoke about the art, Dave Jackson told Rick, "We're here to blend, to join, to lead each other. You have to want that, even when you don't see it happening." Which at first meant almost nothing to Rick when Dave Jackson grabbed an arm and fixed a choke-hold around Rick's neck so his shoulders tensed with the desperate need to free himself from an enemy's grip, a tension which only strengthened Jackson's hold. "Breathe, relax," Dave whispered into his ear. And when he did relax, Dave guided him into a duck-and-glide that released him effortlessly. Unless, as mostly happened, he tensed again midway in the maneuver and the lock went back on. A hundred times, five hundred times, I watched as Rick fell victim to the desperation of battle, the imperative to kill or be killed as a sudden grab called up the impulse to force his way. Every muscular and emotional habit pushed in that direction: the grinding jaw, the crawl of scalp, the tense forehead,

184

the tightening in back and belly.

When it was Rick's turn to strike at Dave Jackson, his move was intercepted and absorbed by a bear-hug which led to an unresisting fall. He'd look up to see Dave Jackson standing beside his flattened form, waiting for him to get up again and try again, and again be met with an invincible bear hug.

The moment came, a hundred, five hundred times later, when Rick felt the grab and the choke and took it as a signal to relax and find a way to slip out of the grip and bring Dave Jackson himself to a fall. And though the fears and tensions returned, they were also signals to relax into strangely effective movement.

"It feels like I'm stepping back from my own choke-hold," he told Dave Jackson, who nodded in agreement and said something vague about anger management. They were friends now and didn't always need to talk.

CHAPTER 29: CONVERGENCES

CLAIRE LEARNED to spin during those days at May's and Garth's, twisting one end of a length of carded wool around the silver hand, gripping the spindle with her left hand, stretching the slender cloud of wool and drawing it down onto the spindle with the silver hand, the spindle turning in her hand as the wool stretched into yarn that varied in thickness and became more uniform as she practiced.

She tried to ignore the phantom pain with its sharp reminders of loss. My substance echoed her pain, and I wondered how much of it had to do with unseen attitudes of mine still troubling the Thread. But she kept on spinning, and when the skein was thick and full, she and May immersed it in a bronzy-orange dye-bath brewed from onion skins saved from the summer's crop.

There were walks with Ashford, chickens and

sheep to tend, trips to the root cellar to check fermenting beets or ripening cheese. Always, the sense of a joined work with the others.

Claire asked to help in the garden, and May gave her a hoe which grew lighter as her arm muscles firmed. The new strength in her arms harmonized with the silver hand's powerful grip as she cleaned out the chicken coop and grew fond of the chickens, who had names and from whom they collected eggs every day.

One morning at breakfast May said to Garth, "Nonie's stopped laying." He nodded silently, and their conversation moved on to take up matters of the kitchen garden and the sheep pen.

That afternoon, May tucked the chicken they called Nonie under one arm and walked to the big oak behind the house, away from the other chickens and the chicken shed. She held up the bird before the tree, then grasped Nonie's legs in her left hand so the bird dangled head down. In a practiced way, her right hand twisted Nonie's neck so that the bird's upper vertebrae pulled apart and the chicken's head hung loose, her wings flurrying briefly.

May carried the bird toward Claire, who stood transfixed by what she had seen. "Nonie gave us a thousand eggs. And now--chicken for dinner," May said cheerfully.

In the kitchen, she laid the chicken on the work table, and they set about plucking the still warm bird. Claire had the city-dweller's dismay at the unfamiliar task, but the silver hand moved in and plucked with firmness and

187

care until the root of the smallest feather was pinched out. May took the chicken to the sink, cut it open, and they wondered at the sight of an egg lying in the chicken's womb. May bathed the bird in cold water and gave it to Claire to cut up for the pan. In the silver hand, the knife glided effortlessly between bones and sinews, and May said, "You're an old hand at this, aren't you?"

Afterwards, while the chicken simmered in the pot with a clove-studded onion and oregano plucked from the bush by the door, May took two of the bird's feathers and gave Claire one of them. Together they walked back to the tree where the chicken had died. A small breeze passed across the yard and the feathers lifted in flight.

Watching there with Claire and May, I felt our calm connection. And, in the days that followed, the phantom pain was a little quieter. Who knows how these things work?

The season's last chrysanthemums and roses were blooming in the garden which Claire was tending. She paused to admire the blooms' perfection in the wintry sun and thought of the lovely bouquet they would make. Then she heard the click of the pruner, and looked down to see that her hands were full of chrysanthemums and roses, neatly cut by the silver hand.

May said, "I was saving them to take to friends in Schoonerville."

"I'm sorry," Claire said. "I wasn't paying attention." She felt reluctant to lay the blame on the silver hand.

"What's done is done. Might as well arrange them."

A vase was produced, one of those spiked bases for anchoring flowers turned up, and the silver hand fairly leaped to make a splendid Japanese-style arrangement. "Looks like a professional job," Garth said.

A few days later, Garth came home with a tire which matched the others on Claire's car, and when the weekend came and a neighbor could feed the farm animals, they started off, heading for the Bridge Studio near Schoonerville. By then Claire knew May prepared dyes and yarn for the weaving there.

"They're coming together," I said to the Animals. "Rick on the estate, and Claire going to the weaving studio, which turns out to be on the estate. Quite a coincidence."

"These things happen when they're needed. Of course, they have to be noticed, *Quawwkk*."

We were near the fishing hole by the stream where Candace and I often met. She came running up, out of breath, her dance skirt rippling about her.

"Grandpa! Come look. You have to see this. It's uncle sour guy. Come!"

I wondered what W. C. had gotten himself into. "I hope he's behaving himself," I told her. "If he isn't, I want you to tell me."

"Hurry, Grandpa!"

We came into the Lodge, a comfortable log dwelling not far from the stream and the golf course. People were coming in off the links, ordering brews at the bar. W. C. Fields and the Minimal guy sat in one corner, and right next to W. C., gazing at him with admiration, was a

189

beautiful woman with dark hair, a sensuous body, and the unforgettable face of Hedy Lamarr. It was like seeing Snow White with a couple of the dwarfs.

"Isn't she lovely?" Candace breathed.

The three of them—W.C., Minimal Man, and Hedy Lamarr—were engrossed in diagrams and mathematical formulas covering the table at which they sat. They took turns jotting down numbers and symbols in spare corners of the diagrams.

Minimal Man jumped up and went to the piano, a sturdy black upright, and, looking at the formulas, played a sequence of chords involving rapid changes of key and evoking sequences of emotion—joy, awe, sorrow, praise. I was reminded of the time on the Other Side when I'd heard and recorded the strange series of harmonies at the psychic's demonstration.

W.C. crowed. "Good job, buddy!" The Minimal man beamed. "No jamming and really wide distribution, maybe a few light years out. It's Hedy's invention, to the super-power!"

W.C. wrote in more numbers, and Hedy gave him another of those adoring looks, adding her own equation, to which Minimal Man appended a footnote. W.C. leaned over and almost hugged Hedy, then high-lighted their teamwork with a star flowing golden from his pen.

CHAPTER 30: WEAVING

WITH ASHFORD between us, Claire and I walked behind Garth and May into the long building that stretched across the creek. We came into a light-filled space with large windows, where six wooden frame looms, nearly ceiling high, held partly completed weavings. At the far end of the room a curtained-off space held beds where Claire and May would sleep, with Garth going off to work on a "project."

A tall, rather gaunt woman in jeans and a colorful shirt rose from one of the looms. "Claire Court? I'm Jean Harmon. Welcome." She took Claire's hand. "I hear you've been working your way up here." She gave May a hug. Ashford trotted over, wagging his tail, and got petted.

A kettle was steaming, and the women sat down for tea at a table near the back of the studio. "Here we are in California," Jean said, "trying to work with nomad designs from the Near East. In a way, you can't. We're not in Afghanistan or Persia or the Caucasus. We're working with different sheep, different wool, different plants for dye."

"But the designs?" Claire asked. "Can't they be the same?"

"Not really. When I look at an old weaving, I can't just copy. There's something coming from the weaver that won't let me. When she ran out of a color she took another color and kept on weaving. So the gold dragon grew an orange leg. She improvised. It's something we can learn from her."

They sat down together at a loom holding a half-finished rug. A drawing pinned to the frame of the loom showed a diagonal pattern moving up to the center of the weaving, then down toward the blue border of the design. They'd work together on the rug, Jean said.

"I'm slow at knotting," Claire apologized in advance as her left hand moved hesitantly to place a length of scarlet yarn between the vertical warp threads. Meanwhile Jean knotted her way skillfully across the threads and was rapidly nearing the middle of the weaving where her work would meet Claire's.

"I used to wear a mirror on the stump to fool the phantom hand into thinking it was being useful," Claire said.

"Why fool a hand that isn't there into thinking it is?"

"It seemed practical, given the pain, but it never did much good." The unhappiness of the lost hand seared through her for the thousandth time.

Jean arrived at the middle of the row and waited for Claire to finish her half so that a long weft thread could be sent across the loom and pounded into place before they started on the next row of knots. Claire struggled, feeling her awkwardness. One knot, then two. The two hands weren't in synch yet, she told herself. They needed time to come together.

"You *are* a bit slow," Jean said. "Why don't you try to go twice as fast?"

"I don't like to hurry."

"I don't mean *hurry*."

The silver hand could easily move twice as fast as the pace that felt normal to Claire. But speeding up made her tense. She didn't want the hand to rush ahead on its own: the rug they were working on wasn't parsnips or chrysanthemums.

And the lost hand kept begging for attention, crying out from some prison where it lay gripped and suffering.

CHAPTER 31: THE CRAFT OF ENTERING

THE ANIMALS keep track of my experiments with the tree and the rock, and now one of the adolescent hawks we've been observing for weeks is flexing his wings. Dog tells me I am ready to enter the bird. But on his maiden flight? I'm used to traveling with my guides and sliding along the Thread, but Entering is different. How can I go inside this inexperienced creature and lift into the sky with nothing to hold me up? I don't have a body, but I'm still afraid of falling. Blame it on Mason.

"We're not nearly the right size," I complained. Dog's look told me it was a matter of adapting, of getting small enough to fit into a rabbit hole, or into the rabbit itself--or a half-grown hawk. I didn't like the idea of being so small. Body stuff again, helpless claustrophobia.

"Enter. *Now*."

A yearning vibration sang along the filament, and the young hawk waited, ready to receive me. And then I was inside him, looking out through his eyes with their keen binocular vision, sensing his quick heartbeat and the stretch of his wings. Two in one, we rose into the intensity of air, sunlight, sky.

Except that it didn't happen. Fear seized me again, and I held back. Who was I to fly, and in an inexperienced bird?

I watched beside the Animals as the young hawk lifted into the air without me, his eager wings beating. But you must work hard to stay airborne till you get to soaring or at least gliding altitude. I'd learned that in my trips with Mallard, but Hawkling didn't know that yet, and his wingbeat was not vigorous enough. He tumbled into a pile of fir needles, and his watchful parents flew down to him.

"Let them handle this," Dog said. Hawkling would need protection and coaching, and my own attempts needn't clog the situation.

I'd failed again. "I'm sorry," I told the Animals. Once again they seemed unconcerned.

"That was a lovely, true Imaging," Mallard said. "Now you know how we live. You know what flying is like."

"But I didn't fly."

"You will."

The Animals told me more about the Entering,
195

which shamans have practiced for thousands of years. They've flown with eagles, prowled with lions. For the Entering to take place, you can't cling to a body's beliefs in permanence and separation and solidity. You must let those go. Or swallow them whole. Then you can become transparent enough to Enter.

I am losing my habit of assuming that I still have a body and the fear that goes with that. The remaining tatters with their merde-brown hue have acquired a few rainbow flecks. The bowing, as I get better at remembering it, helps too. It tilts me toward a new respect, and I was grateful to the young hawk for the willingness I'd felt in him. Even though I'd backed off.

In the weaving studio, Claire looked at the half-finished pieces on the looms, handsome rugs boldly patterned. She recognized designs from areas in the vast region from the Amu Darya in the north to the Zagros mountains in the south, from Baluchi territory in the east, to the Caucasus far to the west.

Years before, she had seen a movie filmed in the hills and remote villages of Afghanistan. The film showed women weaving bright rugs and saddlebags, protective hangings for doorways, and rectangles of fine weaving on which to place food for an honored guest. The people's eyes and leathery faces held lifetimes of journeys to and from upland pasture, moving from winter to summer and back again. Not long after the film was made, the Russians invaded the country and there followed a great wiping-out of traditional life.

Afghanistan had been penetrated by war many times before, but this time the amount of destruction had multiplied and much was gone--trees and soil, songs and patterns, customs and allegiances. After seeing the film, Claire dreamed that somewhere, in a hidden valley, traditions were preserved, like vanished birds still singing somewhere.

She noticed a half-woven rug with strong, sturdy borders. Jean said, "Maria's working on that one." At that moment, they heard steps on the deck leading into the workshop, and Maria came in. Claire wondered: Was she half-Tibetan or three-quarters Irish? Spanish or Indian? Gorgeous anywhere.

"I'll be away for an hour or two," Jean said. "And May's cooking up a dye batch. Why don't the two of you work together?" Claire and Maria exchanged smiles, women at the beginning of relationship.

I waited for Claire's recognition of Maria, but it didn't happen. It occurred to me they had never met; there'd been the sequestering of mother and child, and then the disaster of Elena's abduction and death. Judy had asked her mother to stay away from a dangerous situation. Claire heard radio reports but never saw a photograph of Maria.

As they worked together at the loom, the younger woman slowed her pace to match Claire's slower tempo. Maria waited quietly for Claire to finish her part of the knotted row, while Claire sensed Maria's quickness and the gap between their ways of working.

197

During my long nights of watching on the estate, I look in on the sleepers. You can go into a dream from This Side without the Entering which goes deeper and is a delicate intimate thing. Maria's sleep, like Rick's, is interrupted by restless dreams and abrupt waking. She tries not to disturb Jean, who shares a room with her, but the same dream unrolled before my eyes and filled the room whenever I happened to be there--the pressing down of a man's heavy body, the violent forcing, the warnings about keeping silent. And there was a child in her dreams--a little girl who stared at her from a cold and scary place.

Rick's situation isn't anything I mess with — the agonizing experiences repeated over many months. And now he and Dave Jackson are training together in the late afternoons, working with new habits of response that trace fresh neural pathways in Rick's brain and body.

Though I'm staying out of Rick's subconscious, it could be useful to go into Maria's dreams to suggest ways she could free herself from their spell. I've thought of different possibilities: a stout staff and the hearty will of an ancient woman warrior, body armor which could envelop her at the man's touch and allow her to spring away from him, changing into a wriggling snake that disappears into the floorboards.

But what did I understand about the psyche of a woman who'd been so mistreated? I sensed my old compulsion to "make things work out" and pulled back from those schemes. In the end, though, I couldn't resist leaving a prop which she might or might not notice.

Remembering how important it had been for Claire to drive again after she'd lost her hand, I deposited a miniature black roadster in one corner of the dream, a sleek convertible which the dreamer might enlarge and whiz away in. I hoped she would like the car, and I considered returning to leave increasingly delightful models. I even imagined riding in the passenger's seat beside Maria, with the top down under the stars.

Mallard appeared, her beak awry with concern. "A black car? Oh, my dear." She produced an image of Arnold Warp's black car, and I withdrew the convertible. In its place, miniaturized in a corner, I left a sturdy palomino pony that Maria might want to ride away on when she was ready.

"Lucy's getting old," Jean said to Walt Adams. "She won't always be able to keep the pigs away."

"Getting old *again*?"

"She needs to train the new Lucy, Time we found her a pup."

"All right, Dave Jackson can work on it, maybe the new man."

The nearest breeder, a woman in Almador, told Dave when he called that there wasn't much demand for Ridgebacks; they were working dogs who needed a lot of exercise, not suburban pets. They didn't fit into most places unless a serious watchdog was needed. You've got that requirement? Well then, he was invited to view her current pups, six females, five males. Ridgebacks had good-sized litters.

Dave drove to Almador and spotted the new Lucy right away, bold and nosy, stepping over her littermates to check him out, insisting he pay attention to her. Dave brought her back with him to the estate, leaving her in the crate until the elder Lucy could get acquainted. Which happened when the pup trotted out of the crate and Lucy licked her all over.

"Now this puppy can't be a plaything," the old man told them. "She's going to be a working dog. It's up to Lucy to train her and up to us to see that she does."

Maria took a liking to the new Lucy, and Jean chided the three of them about picking the pup up--and knew they were doing it when she wasn't looking. And talk--- there are so many things to be said when you have a puppy to look after.

Maria and Claire were alone in the workshop, Jean having gone off to wherever she went. They sat at the loom side by side, each knotting half a row, meeting in the middle. Claire had just received an email from Judy reciting her frustration at the lack of progress in finding Rick Mendoza, and she paused, still lost in Judy's exasperation, while Maria waited silently for her to complete the knot. *She has to wait for me*, Claire realized, sensing Maria's brisk rhythm and the silver hand's eagerness to match it. A new willingness appeared in her, and she quickened her pace to blend with Maria's tempo. For several rows, they knotted in harmony.

"You've found a way to work together," May said, as

she came in with a handful of dark roots.

Sometimes we met in the mountains above the old man's place, not far from the western boundary of the estate. The Animals liked to keep vigil there, though it was the side of the estate you would think was already well protected. A ridge descended to where the sea struggled against cliffs along the coast, with only a narrow highway making its way above the shore. Some lone cabins, a hamlet or two, not much else; no obvious reason to watch up there. But the site had plenty of exposure to the changes of weather the sea winds carried inland, and the Animals seemed interested in such changes. Subtle shadings of color, shifts in the wind, the grumble of rocks high in the mountains--they were sensitive to all these. And maybe human weather, too, like the presence of powerful interests in skyscrapers in San Francisco and Los Angeles, New York, and Beijing, making plans which could result in exploding mountain tops and dried-up rivers.

Ashford and Claire took a daily walk after breakfast. Mornings were clear in the inland valley, unlike the city where they waited for their walk until the fog lifted, or accepted that it wasn't going to lift and they might as well go anyway. At first, they took the walks Jean pointed out, up a nearby hill, or along a trail circling through the woods or leading to Sweetfalls Creek.

One morning Ashford followed a new route and they came to the locked wrought-iron gate that led to the estate. When Claire asked about it, Jean said it was

201

private property owned by a big landowner, Walt Adams. A day or two later, she saw Jean approaching from the other side of the gate, opening it, and proceeding toward the weaving studio. Ashford ran up to her and Jean bent to pet him, then moved on in silence. Claire figured she might be told something later. Or not.

Occasionally May went off to spend time with Garth. Maria came and went unpredictably. More unanswered questions.

During the night, I visited the sleepers as they dreamed. As I listened beside Claire, her right arm throbbed, still unreconciled to separation from the lost hand, and I worried that the severed arm might still cause trouble. I would have comforted her but didn't know how. Watching was acceptable, I told myself. But no messages. I wasn't going to fall into that mind-trap again. I stayed beside her, sensing something lacking that wasn't physical at all.

With Rick, it was the same. Loss and despair filled his dreams, as though a vital part had been torn out of him in the Afghan mountains. Working with Dave Jackson, he was paying attention to the martial art's demand to relax in moments of threat and danger, but his dreams didn't reflect that.

When I met with the Animals, I said, "Claire and Rick have a lot in common. Something's gone missing for them both."

Dog looked interested. I continued, "Claire's right hand is missing, but it's more than that. They've both got a big hole inside." I struggled with a word I wasn't accustomed to using, "It's like they're missing parts of their souls. Parts that couldn't bear what was happening and ran away."

Dog nodded. "Anywhere in all the worlds."

I remembered accounts of shamans who go into trance states to hunt for missing souls. They search through the universe and battle demons to rescue the lost ones and bring them back to the bodies they have left.

I felt a huge wish for Rick and Claire and longed to search for what was missing in them.

"The seeker may become lost himself." Dog presented the image of a puzzled traveler wandering among the deceptive curtains of the aurora.

Mallard broke in. "But it can be done. With quickness and courage. With boldness." Her speckled breast expanded almost to bursting.

"I want to try."

Dog said, "Perhaps you may.

"*Quarrrrk*. He even has a Call. . . "

"When do I start?"

They left the question hanging in the sky over the estate.

CHAPTER 32: GLIMPSES AND DISTURBANCES

JUDY WAS UNHAPPY. Rick the murderer had vanished, the "all points alert" was without result. "Enough," she said to Greg. "We're going to hire a detective. Now."

"What about your mom? Maybe you should talk to her first."

"She's off by herself, doing her thing. I'm not sure she's interested."

"All right. I'll find a decent operative."

"Decent meaning competent?"

"I'll find someone who knows his business."

I regretted Judy's insistence on playing her hand. The connections to her mother's blood supply needed gentle handling. I had been instructed to keep track of both Rick and Claire, which hinted that bad things might happen if there was serious interference. Even nonviolent interventions, like my spirit-writing attempts, had been disruptive. Still, Judy's intentions were good. She wanted to help. I did too, which for both of us was an old and treacherous feeling.

It occurred to me to do another dream visit, the least intrusive move I could think of. I didn't want to strengthen Judy's resistance to even sensible suggestions, so I didn't plan to show up in her subconscious. Greg, though, was a candidate for a straightforward visit. We had always gotten along, and it was in his nature to see more than one side of things.

Moving into someone's dream is a smooth enough thing, and I slid down a palm frond to where Rick stood in his swim trunks on the Big Island.

He seemed glad to see me. "I'm all right," I told him. "I'm in a good place. I've made friends."

"That's great," he said.

"I'd like you to be aware of something," I went on. "The vet, Rick Mendoza, who killed me, is working on himself. I've forgiven him. It won't help to send him to jail. Can you get Judy to call off the detective?" He smiled, turned, and stepped into a Coast Guard patrol plane that swooped away.

I was yanked out of the dream, bumped down at the edge of the clearing where we often met. Dog, Mallard, and Raven were there, and I waited for some reprimand. But they communicated among themselves and seemed unaware of my presence.

"It's coming closer," Dog was saying. "He'll need to stay with the View as if his life depended on it."

"His life?" croaked Raven.

"Whatever he holds dear," Dog replied. "Whatever he's connected to."

They turned, noticing me and looking genuinely surprised. I wondered if I had been honored by some other, more urgent pull.

Back at the estate, I had glimpses:

Rick and Maria standing outside the kitchen, Maria turning away from him. Has Rick Done Something?

Fear turns her away, Mallard whispered.

Maria and Claire, weaving together. "What's it like not to have a hand?" Maria asks.

"You have to listen to it cry."

"Will it always cry?"

"I hope not." Claire closed her eyes as the phantom pain stabbed into her spine. Then she went back to work on Maria's border, a repeating trefoil design which alternated between dark and light. Sometimes the light dominated the pattern, and sometimes the dark.

Brad Pointer seemed mostly dark to me, not well blended, and I didn't understand why he was allowed on the estate. He was local, from Schoonerville, and hung out with the Schoonerville police. In an all-points alert, Rick's blurred picture, sans the beard he'd grown, might have aroused a question in Pointer.

He and Rick crossed paths one Saturday morning at the gabions. Pointer was cascading a load of rocks into a half-filled gabion when Rick came up the stream with a sack full of stones, limping a little as he walked on the uneven stream bed. "What's the matter with your leg?"

Pointer asked. "Have an accident?"

Rick nodded curtly, keeping busy unloading the sack. "A while back. It's healing."

"Get rammed by someone? Or was it the other way around?"

Just then Dave Jackson gave a call for Rick to look at something downstream, and Rick, his sack emptied, moved away without replying. Brad Pointer took out his cell phone, riffling through photos and web sites and staring hard after Rick.

"That guy is going to mess things up," I said to the Animals.

But they brushed off my concerns, treating me like someone who doesn't understand how things work.

CHAPTER 33: THE DETECTIVE

THE DETECTIVE, Mike Harrison, was also a CPA, riding to his appointments with small businesses in his state-of-the-art Harley Davidson. Socializing with casual friends along Route 1 and Route 5, he had become familiar with much of the state. Over coffee or a beer, he would draw the conversation in the direction of a current investigation, learning what the locals knew. In this case, he would be conducting a search for Rick Mendoza, as requested by the lawyer Greg Lathrop, and also by Mrs. Judy Lathrop, with whom he had a pointed conversation in which she made clear she was primarily interested in results. *Find this guy.*

The Animals sent me pointers: note the detective's lively buzz of a brain, his quick body, his alertness even when he's had a couple of beers. Their advice was hardly needed, for I liked what I sensed about him--that he was not easy to fool, kept on asking questions and checking out responses. He was a fellow skeptic, an advanced one.

After speaking with Sylvia and hearing about their childhood at the Christmas tree farm, the detective headed north, reviewing his options. Each part of the state meant something different, both for a fugitive and his pursuer. Finding someone in Humboldt county, with its armed thickets of marijuana, differed from finding someone in the grasslands hemming the sea along the Mendocino coast, or in the Klamath river area, where threatened rivers ran between barren hills. Inland, toward Mt. Lassen and its cinder cones, sometimes just a scrim of trees screened a clear-cut.

In the part of California where he thought Rick might be hiding, the Christmas tree farm drew the detective like a magnet.

The woman at the tree farm told him about the dark-haired young man who was a nephew of the people who used to own the place and had spent summers there as a kid. He had a limp but was otherwise able-bodied.

Their conversation turned to the detective's itinerary. Mike Harrison said, "A couple of years ago I thought I'd ride the Harley up into the back country, But the road gave out at a locked gate."

The woman nodded. "You came to the Adams estate. Sometimes there's a polite person turning people away like what they do down the coast at the Bohemian Grove."

"Yeah. Polite but firm, and that's as far as you get."

Young people found work on the property, she said,

and old Walt Adams kept it from the wrong kind of development. "He got some kind of message overseas, came back from Vietnam, and started to improve the land."

"He doesn't get much publicity."

"Or want it. You won't find the old man on Facebook."

"A man with that kind of property isn't too bad for the local economy," the detective said.

"He grows a lot of his own food, but the feed store and the hardware store get plenty of his business, too. Jim Hagerty at the feed store makes a trip out there every few days."

The Harley's engine felt a little rough, the detective told the garage owner, a man in his sixties who knew how to work on motorcycles. The detective said he would like to take it as far out the back roads as he could. "Though it gets hard to navigate the back roads around here. I ran into a locked gate a couple of times."

"Well, if you're interested in exploring, check in with Jim Hagerty. He's in his delivery truck delivering feed during the week but on weekends he takes off on his motorbike. He can point you to dirt roads you might try without running up against the Adams estate, which I guess is what you mean."

The garage man started up the Harley's motor and said, "If I were heading into the woods, I would tune down that muffler some."

"Take her down as far as you want." The detective strolled over to the feed store, where Jim Hagerty got out his topo map and did some pointing and tracing with his index finger.

A patrol car stopped in front of the feed store. A man in a black uniform and silver badge got out, greeted Jim Hagerty and eyed the detective. He was looking, he said, for a young guy, bearded, a scar on his left cheek, who might have come through town looking for a ride. He had skipped bail a while back, and the San Francisco authorities were raising a ruckus about finding him. He flashed a picture of Rick.

Hagerty said he hadn't seen Rick. "And I'm too old to be the guy you're describing," the detective said.

The patrol car drove off. Jim Hagerty spit into the gravel. "A little lie never hurt with him."

"A little lie?"

"Or a moderate sized one," he said, returning the detective's gaze. "City labels don't fit out here. I like to get my own sense of people, and if someone wants to hitch a ride with me, I don't check the wanted posters first. Now Curly there," a nod toward the departing police officer, "is quick to figure out which side his bread is buttered on, and he'll tell you the other side is covered with rat poison. I like to make up my own mind about these things."

"I like to do that too," the detective said. "Of course, it doesn't hurt to be able to defend yourself in case things take a different turn. Looks like you could." He eyed Jim Hagerty's capable-looking frame.

"Self-defense training is a good idea," Hagerty said. He said he had learned some footwork in boxing.

211

The detective called the head of the dojo where he taught the Japanese art of aikido to say he would be out of town for a few days. Somebody else would have to cover the Sunday morning practice. "All right," came the reply. "Can you make it back for the *kyu* tests next week?" The detective thought he could.

He headed for the estate. He'd need to find a place to stash the Harley, and then find a way to observe people. It was so often that way: the glamorous life of a detective came down to watching until you saw what you needed to see.

Though clients seldom viewed it that way. They thought along the lines of finding and nabbing, with a short impatient interlude of establishing identity and verifying behavior. In this case, what Mrs. Judy Lathrop wanted was firm identification. Just find him, identify him, inform her, and pick him up. That was it.

It wasn't that easy. People didn't do the expected, and it got complicated. But you had a job to do.

Jim Hagerty had mentioned little-used roads, short cuts through corners of the estate. These were little more than dirt trails but wide enough for the Harley, and the detective found his way. Finally, he stopped the motor, camouflaged the Harley, and moved quietly on foot, taking note of how water and bird sounds gradually mingled with human voices and the sounds of tools. He noticed the unusual treatment of trees near the water's edge, how saddle-shaped posts supported their drooping branches.

The detective was close to what he figured was the

center of the place, with a big house, sheds, a barn appearing through the trees, when he made a discovery. High in a big oak with spreading arms, he noticed the edge of a platform, nearly hidden among the leaves, with toeholds in the trunk leading up to it. Somebody's old tree house.

Some of the toeholds on the trunk were missing and others were in disrepair, which made the detective think that unexpected visitors wouldn't be a problem. He nimbly ascended the ladder-like toeholds into the lean of the tree and reached the half-decayed platform that he found could bear his weight. He gave the obscured downward view a discreet trimming with the clippers he carried with him and settled in with his binoculars and camera and the supplies in his backpack. He had a good view of the main house with its kitchen entrance and, on one side, an open grass-covered space.

It might take a few days to see whatever he needed to see, ascending the platform at daybreak and leaving after dark to find his way back to the Harley. But the view from there was a good one. He tossed down the remains of a sandwich to the big yellow dog that came up growling softly, accepting the offering.

CHAPTER 34: MY JOURNEY

SINCE HIS FIRST LIFT-OFF, the young hawk's parents have guarded him as he grows and develops a sharp warning call like theirs. I've joined him every day in the layer of needles and reminded him of that first lift into the air, which would only grow in power. *You'll do it again*, I tell him. He flaps his wings and screams a warrior-like "kyee." Still, I might not be along for his next lift-off, for a few nestlings have remained above him in the tree, and one of them might be chosen for me.

Today, as I joined the Animals at the ancient cypress, Mallard said, "We mustn't wait any longer." A single adolescent had occupied the nest the day before. Now he was gone, and the nest was empty.

Dog pointed to Hawkling, whose splotchy white and beige feathers had turned tawny orange and brown. "He's ready."

Mallard agreed, bobbing her beak in the bird's direction.

Suddenly I felt hesitant. Why couldn't I enter a bird who hadn't screwed up? But Raven gave me a long stare.

All right. I'll go.

"Watch everything," Dog said. "Expect nothing."

The filament throbbed with longing, and I bowed to Hawkling as he stood in the pile of fir needles. He worked his wings up and down in a confident way. *Yessir, we're meant to fly.* I bowed to him again and felt again the yearning of the Filament. And now was my time. The only time.

So I slipped into him, aligning my substance with his head and backbone and heart. With a revving of wings that took us well above the topmost branch of the cypress, we rose into the air.

High above the trees, our keen shared eyes probed the landscape below us with the frontal gaze which hawks and humans have. Hawkling carried in his genes ancestral migration maps, but even they couldn't tell him where to find the lost souls of Rick and Claire. And I didn't know where to search either. But we looked for clues, zooming down to investigate features of the landscape.

Hints appeared. A trace of Claire's lost hand--a red-fingered print on a pale eucalyptus trunk--appeared at the edge of a vast plain. A battered poster tacked to the side of a barn pictured a small boy with dark straight hair beside a Christmas tree. Characters who seemed to

215

think it was their job to delay us, to circumvent, re-route, and deceive guarded those places. Some wore knee pants and hose and shoes with ornate buckles and shouted warnings in antiquated Spanish. Others — stern-looking women and bearded sailors — had a New England look.

Who were these creatures guarding the woods and caves and harbors which Hawkling soared toward and inspected? How complex the ancient confusions must be! Was I being asked to untangle all of this to find the missing parts of Rick and Claire?

We faced storms that threw Hawkling off course, trips into the burning heart of the earth, a sliding off the face of the cold moon as earthrise appeared, each time the wrong-place-wrong-time giving a new direction for the search. Guardians and fierce defenders challenged us and let us pass, as we met them with threatening beak and keen claws.

Wraith-like beings slept, then reared up with terrible shouts that woke other sleepers. I would have quickly flown past them, but I remembered Dog's instruction and observed them too. At which they relapsed into torpor or vanished.

At last we came to a narrow crevasse deep in barren mountains. There, two children clung to the mangled metal encasing them. The girl's bony, reddened right hand was bigger than it should have been; the boy, tormented by the cruelly twisted steel, wept and shouted, reached out for the girl's hand, never could touch it. A murky dust of decay and repression

216

darkened the nearly airless space in which the children coughed and choked. Both wore masks that hid their faces--hers a wriggling mass of fingers, his that of a sullen, frightened warrior.

I stepped out of my presence in Hawkling and walked toward them, my footsteps raising clouds of dust. "Rick, Claire. I've come for you. It's time to go home." They paused in their endless writhing. "You don't need those," I said, pointing to the masks they clutched to their hidden faces.

Hawkling offered his beak and claws to free them, but Claire screamed in pain as he struck at the metallic tangle, and I called out for him to stop. Rick did not move, his angry shouting replaced by dull passivity. They made a frozen tableau, with Claire fearing to move, weeping soundlessly, and Rick motionless and withdrawn.

I drew closer to them and was horrified to see drops of what looked like blood falling on Claire's hand. Someone else was caught in the murderous tangle, someone whose blood rained down on Claire.

CHAPTER 35: THE WISH FOR HOME

HE WORE NO MASK, and I was looking at a part of myself which had fled from the chaos of the accident. Through the tangle of metal, bloody drops misted from his pores and fell endlessly on Claire's hand.

"John," I said to him. "Come out of there. Now. It's time to return."

He eyed me suspiciously. "No. I've got to keep giving Claire blood or she'll bleed to death. I can't let that happen."

"Claire's hand is all right," I told him. 'Look." But he gave only a brief unseeing glance. "I have to give her my blood," he repeated.

"Can't you see she doesn't need your blood?"

I blessed the skeptic in him for showing up in time to recognize that Claire's arm and hand were whole and that she had turned with yearning toward the promised ride on Hawkling.

"Come on, all of you," I said. "Time for the ride home."

They protested: "We're trapped. We can't get out."

"Remember you want to be home," I said, catching the deep wish in their eyes. "This place is not what you think it is. If you want to be free, look again, and you'll see you *are* free."

We tried together. I shared their perception of trapping and imprisonment and their joy as the view cleared and widened, the canyon walls parted and the sky seeped in. The metal tangle shifted and softened. Vises and clamps and twisted wire offered openings the right size for arms, heads, trunks, and legs to squeeze through, and in a moment the lost ones were free.

Stars shimmered through the murk and Hawkling's glance poured over them. His wings, like the silken sleeve of a Kwan Yin, brushed lightly over them. Their masks dropped away, and they were eager to rejoin the rest of themselves. The part of me trapped with them didn't have to wait: my substance opened and he came back inside, at the level of the heart.

I was ready to re-enter Hawkling, and told the children about the thrilling ride they would have on his back. But the boy Rick said, "No, there's someone else. We have to find her." Her name was Maria, he said.

Hawkling lifted us into the sky and the search resumed, until far below we spotted a densely-wooded island, rimmed with cliffs above which a dark cloud churned. Half visible through the cloud, dark shapes swarmed, cloddish but of human form. They wore animal masks--distorted tigers, lions, hyenas--that I recognized as symbols of a cult which had usurped the more benign healing traditions of the islands where Arnold Warp grew up. Masks intended to ward off sickness were perverted into symbols of revenge and cruelty. And now they blocked a path which led into the woods of the island. "She's in there," Rick said.

Hawkling flew toward another entrance into the woods, but the swarm spotted us and surged toward us. A huge shape, wearing a snarling bear-mask, bristling with axes and knives, hurtled in my direction, so loaded down that inertia carried it past me as I leaped to one side.

The bear mask came toward me again, and I swerved past him so that by the time he slowed down I was again out of his reach. And now more figures separated from the swarm and moved toward us-- toward me and toward Claire and Rick, whose childlike souls were quicker than any mask wearer. They leaped and glided and swooped out of the reach of the clumsy creatures.

But it wouldn't be enough. We'd keep avoiding them and they'd keep coming back at us. I remembered Dog's rendition of Cerberus, the fierce guardian of the Greek afterlife. At the time, I hadn't understood what Dog was getting at, but I did now, and wished mightily to present myself as Cerberus, or his equivalent, before those howling masked despoilers. I had promised to bring back the children and I wished hard for whatever would allow me to keep my promise. Maybe not Cerberus, I

220

wasn't insisting on him, but some Power that was available and finer than anything our crude attackers had. As the next brute came toward me, I bowed to the possibility. Then I was towering over the dark masked form, sending my arms out in a gesture like thunder. I'm not sure what he saw--maybe Thor or some temple guardian from the Far East. Or Cerberus.

It worked. The attackers fled to shelter in the dark cloud, and the swarm moved away. I stood in full Menace until they had all disappeared.

Free to search again, we entered the wood, searching for Maria's missing soul. Deep in the forest we found a cottage, where a beautiful woman sat at a loom weaving beside another weaver, a little girl: Maria and her daughter, Elena.

Maria said the weaving would be a shawl for Elena. "It's nearly finished," she said. She seemed frightened, and I wondered if she unraveled the weaving the way you'd set back a clock, not wanting it to be completed.

Elena gave a little girl's rustle of independence and got up from the loom "Mama, here's God. He's found us!"

Crack! Suddenly a whip lashed out, and a formidable creature appeared, grotesque, with eyeballs dangling from their sockets and a thicket of bristling black hair. He wore the cheap costume of a Halloween pirate, the kind you find in dollar stores by late September, and my suspicions grew. The whip snaked and snapped toward Maria, who drew back in terror.

Then the apparition ripped off its mask, and Arnold

221

Warp stood framed in the doorway of Maria's cottage. Hungry-looking beasts thronged around him — surly lions, evil-eyed hyenas, jackals nipping at each other. Outside, Warp's black limousine purred up to the cottage, driven by a chauffeur who was chained to the steering wheel.

Warp stretched his face into a slick smile. "Let's go, you two." He held out a box of expensive chocolates to Maria and Elena. "Enjoy these on the ride home. Nobody has the right to take you away from me, do you hear that, Maria?" Warp cracked the whip in the direction of his chauffeur, and the man was freed from the steering wheel. He emerged from the car and opened the rear door.

"Get in, *now*," Warp ordered.

Maria stood motionless and bewildered. But Elena stepped forward and boldly faced Warp, growing in stature until she stood before him at eye level. Sparks of energy crackled from her fingertips.

"You're not my real dad," she said. "You aren't going to hurt me again, and you're not going to hurt Mama any more."

She picked up the wooden shuttle of the loom, and it grew in her hand until it became a wand of power. Warp swore and grabbed for her, but she veered off. Then Elena ran toward him, touched him with the shuttle, and Warp shrank into the body of a five-year-old who screamed and stamped and was powerless against the Presence who stood before him.

The five-year-old cracked his whip at the chauffeur,

222

who saluted and climbed back into his chains. Then Warp dived into the Beemer and the car pulled away, the miserable child inside it screaming orders to his servant.

After I assured Maria that the rest of her was lonely without her, she and Elena climbed in front of Rick onto Hawkling's back. I re-entered him and we swept into the sky.

We didn't go directly back to the estate, for lost souls must be prepared for their return to the human state, the way a diver needs to be lifted slowly to the ocean's surface. We came back to a place where the Animals waited for us beside a warming fire, and where we listened to the stories they told. They recited tales of falsity unveiled, of girls with no hands redeemed by love, of the deathless friendship of warriors. Of lost children who found their way from danger to safety. Stories with meanings that opened and blossomed as they were told and retold. I listened too and felt the stories settling into me like medicine.

In that time, near Raven, Mallard and Dog, the children Rick and Claire bloomed. Maria, with Elena beside her, grew more confident about returning to the fullness of human life. My own soul settled into place on This Side, in the Completing which is never quite complete.

"What about Arnold Warp?" I asked the Animals. What kind of lost soul is he?"

Mallard quacked softly. "Almost entirely lost," she said. "There's not much left for him to come back to."

"*Quawwkk.* And not much interest in rescuing him, either."

Mallard looked a little sad. "Surely there's always *some.*"

"And what about Elena? What a terrific kid! How did she get to be that way?"

It was a matter of lineage, Dog let me know. I glimpsed a line of Elenas going far, far back.

Though we seemed to spend months and years listening to the stories the Animals told, the moon had just risen when Hawkling and I returned to the estate, bringing their lost parts to Rick and Claire and Maria. Rick woke inside his dream and rose to meet his younger self, who blended into him until the grown Rick took on stature and wholeness. Claire rose from her dream to stand in moonlight, watching the lost hand turn toward the silver hand and stroke its polished surface, warming it, blending itself with it, freed from pain. The silver hand was now blessed with the shape of a woman's hand, its fingers capable of graceful movement. And so it would seem to Claire, for the lost hand now so melded with the silver hand that its form no longer mattered. And the silver hand was gentled in its keenness.

Maria stood in her dream, standing beside Elena, holding her hand. Dog was there, letting her know she had kept faith with her child, and it was time to let Elena go, for she mustn't be kept from Beginning again.

"Mama, I want to ride the horse!" Elena said. She'd seen the fine pony I'd put into her mother's dream. "I know how, I do!"

"By yourself? Alone?"

"I'm going to find my friends!"

Maria kissed Elena and watched as her daughter rode off on the palomino. Claire was comforting her as I tiptoed out of their dreams, our night journey over. The Animals stood in their places by the Rock and the Tree and silently welcomed me, Raven allowed me a croak of commendation. Hawk, no longer Hawkling, stood proudly on that most ancient of beings, the Rock.

Imagine, if you will, the expression on W. C. Fields' face when Candace and Elena descended on him with their invitations to play. At first, he displayed his usual show of stupefied dissatisfaction. Then he saw Elena and seemed confused, until his face cleared and he gave her an unbelievably welcoming smile. "She looks like me," he said. "There's a family resemblance."

"Are you God, too?" she asked.

"Uncle God." He brought out his juggling equipment and began circulating six balls at once, while she balanced on the prancing palomino and skillfully joined the play of juggled balls.

I objected. Elena didn't need boozy comedians in her life. How could W.C. possibly fit into a situation which still ached with horror and loss? But Mallard let me know that Elena and W.C. were a Gloriously Mis-Matched Paradoxical Pair. Mallard demonstrated what that meant, doing a comical dance with Raven while Elena and Candace rocked in cleansing laughter.

225

"They're all crazy," I said to Dog, who simply kept on watching.

CHAPTER 36: "WE'RE RELATED"

IT WAS early Saturday morning. I watched while Rick and Dave Jackson loaded gabions in the creek bed near the Bridge studio. They worked well together now, with a joined sense of the rhythms of stones and water. They joked that the rocks let them know, that a sense of "pick me up" and sometimes "leave me here" came to them, through their hands and the soles of their rubber boots. As they collected stones, they filled gabions in the bank that supported the weaving studio, where a couple of the old man's propped trees grew by the front door of the studio and sank roots into the stream bank.

Rain, cold and hard, pelted them, and Jean came out of the studio and beckoned them up into the warmth. They came in, with quick friendly glances between Maria and Rick. The men sat down, a little awkwardly, while Maria and May brought mugs and cookies and

Jean poured tea.

A woman Rick hadn't seen before came from the back of the studio with a pitcher of milk. "This is Claire Court," Jean said. "She's here to weave with us."

Ashford, who had been snoozing in his bagel-shaped bed, peered out, stretched, sniffed the air, and trotted over to Rick. He put light paws on Rick's knee, his tail wagging hard. In his mouth was the sock, which he'd been keeping beside him. *Here.*

Claire stared at Rick, matching pictures. "He recognizes you. And so do I."

The moment froze around Rick.

"You're Charley's uncle," Claire said. "Sylvia's brother."

Ashford moved on, making the rounds of the tea-drinkers, soliciting pats before ending up at Claire's side.

Jean, who had looked up stories about the accident after Claire had written her, said, "Sylvia? Charley? Aren't they related to . . ." May and Maria looked puzzled.

"It's all right," Claire said. "Yes, they're related. *We're related.*" In her body, I felt the calm pulse of our blood.

"Your name isn't Robert," Jean said to Rick.

Rick nodded, the wave of their recognition pouring over him.

"What now?" I asked Dog. "Will Claire wait to see how things develop? Or decide that she's not so related to Rick after all? Or call Judy?"

"Or," Dog signaled, "none of the above?"

228

Sometimes things get quiet when you think they're about to explode. It was like that on the estate that day. Jean spoke to the old man, who looked as if he couldn't be surprised by much. Then they both went about their business as if nothing was ever final after all and they'd wait for the next thing.

CHAPTER 37: WHAT THE DETECTIVE SAW

IT'S A LONG AFTERNOON for Mike Harrison, watching through his binoculars in the tree house. The rain has stopped, and people are at work, women in the garden, the men in a shed where steel buzzes against wood and hammers pound.

A young guy comes out of the kitchen carrying a plastic bin of what might be garbage. He's of medium height, a dark beard covering his jaw, curly hair. He seems to have a slight limp but the detective can't be sure; carrying a big bin is awkward. There's supposed to be a scar from the accident below his eye, but he doesn't turn his head and the detective can't tell. The beard might be covering it.

The young guy returns with the empty bin just as a beautiful girl walks out of what must be the laundry room, carrying a basket stacked high with folded tablecloths and towels. The detective thinks it likely that yearning vibrations are coming from the guy with the beard, who puts down the bin, walks over to the woman and takes the basket from her with a slight asking, the kind when you're sure someone will be glad of your offer. He takes the basket into the kitchen, then comes out and resumes his task.

They're laying out some mats on the grassy open space. Men and women in training outfits gather, and a man they call Dave demonstrates a martial arts technique, which the others try. The technique, the detective thinks, is not too far from some version of aikido that you run into at one dojo or another.

The bearded guy practices with one partner after another, beginners like him. The limp in his right leg doesn't slow him down, and when he tenses up he lets his shoulders relax. But this is not a situation where he's going to lose it, the others not being much of a challenge. Except for one guy they call Brad, who is more experienced than the others, and whose staring makes "Robert" nervous.

The beautiful girl appears in practice gear and wants to join in. Dave, leading the practice, eases her into a fall, and she comes up from it looking pleased. Before long she goes off the mat, called away by an older woman. The bearded guy watches her go. More yearning.

When they change partners, the rough-looking guy bows briefly to Robert. The next technique involves grabbing your partner hard by the arm. Unless you know better, it's a move guaranteed to call up the

231

instinct to yank yourself out of the situation.

The rough-looking guy is bigger than Robert, and his biceps have been lifting weights. He grabs Robert's forearm, exerting full power, mostly unnecessary. He's not playing the game anymore, not agreeing to yield and fall when he's taken off balance.

The detective sees how Robert tenses, then relaxes and accepts the heavy grip. After that he doesn't do anything. Doesn't resist at all. Keeps on studying the situation and trying to relax.

This goes on for what feels like an hour and might have been two very long minutes. Something distracts the big guy, and his grip relaxes just enough for Robert to send him into a tasty by-the-book fall.

Up in his tree the detective is grinning, and Dave Jackson, who's been watching, looks pleased, too. Meanwhile the other men on the mat have had a chance to do the technique eight or ten times while Robert was waiting out the big guy. It's time to change partners again, and Dave Jackson bows to Robert and takes him for a partner.

This might be different, the detective thinks. Dave Jackson has earned the black belt he wears. And he is up to something. Jackson raises his arm to strike at the bearded guy, but instead grabs his forearm with both hands, not as heavily as the rough guy did. Still, he invites the fight response that is always close to the surface with a guy who's served two tours in Afghanistan. Yet this guy Robert relaxes into the grab enough to make it necessary for Dave Jackson to change

232

his own position. Jackson blocks Robert with a low grip which beginners often try to back out of. Robert doesn't back out, and the detective watches with admiration as Robert springs into a somersault that takes him across the mat, out of Jackson's reach.

Jackson claps his hands, sending everyone into a bow and back to kneeling at the edge of the mat. It's the end of the practice. Dave Jackson turns toward Robert, bowing deeply. As Robert returns the bow, the winter sun lights up the z-shaped scar on his left cheek. The rough-looking guy sees it and files the impression. He exchanges bows with Robert, giving him grudging respect.

The detective has seen enough. After dark, he climbs down from the tree house and makes his way to the Harley, walks it out of the estate and cruises into town. Time for a motel, a shower, a beer. The call to the Lathrops can wait till morning.

Saturday nights were special on the estate. After dinner people gathered for music around the grand piano in the renovated barn. The old man and Jean sat close to the grand piano; the Animals and I listened in back. Garth sat down to play, working from a manuscript with hand-drawn notes, playing music that spoke of longing and joy and sadness. In one of the pieces I recognized the sequence of unusual chords the psychic had written on the blackboard. Now, as Garth improvised, the sequence came alive, connecting the chords into a musical tale filled with strange turnings

233

and reversals, with a not quite harmonious chord at the conclusion—a chord I had puzzled over in the psychic's sketch which seemed to say "To Be Continued."

Afterwards, in the dark of the moon, the Animals and I met on the roof of the weaving studio, with the creek flowing below us and the Rock and the Cypress settling their weight on the stream bank.

My guides weren't relying on words. Listening and a silent language of gesture was enough for them and for me, too. Even the Rock changed its mood as new tints and colors appeared. The tree's gestures changed as the wind moved through its branches in brisk gusts or quiet sighs.

I had questions I wanted to ask--about Rick and Claire. About the blood we shared, its dangers and possibilities. In a few hours, the detective would call Judy and Greg, and soon after the local police station would send a patrol car to the estate; the Schoonerville chief himself might arrive to enjoy the headlines that go with finding an escaped killer. I ballooned out a few images sampling these eventualities, but the Animals ignored them. Yet there was a tension I couldn't interpret in the nervous stir of the Cypress, a minute off-balance in the Rock.

At seven o'clock the next morning, Mike Harrison called Greg and Judy. Greg answered the phone. The detective told him he'd located the missing man, Rick Mendoza, on the Adams estate, a big spread above Mendocino. Making himself useful, evidently.

234

"Trying to get straightened out?" Greg asked.

"You can never be completely sure of that, but it looks like it. He's been working on the estate and training in a martial art I'm familiar with, something you can't do if you give in to the usual fight reactions, especially if you're this guy's size, which is not huge. So, yes, from what I saw he's been working on his issues."

Judy cut in from another phone. "You're sure it's him?"

"All the physical markers fit, Mrs. Lathrop. General appearance, even with the beard he's grown, the Z-scar, the limp. You can call the police either here in San Francisco or up there and have him rounded up."

"Can't you do that?"

The detective paused, then said, "I've found him, Mrs. Lathrop. That's what we agreed on. I have other business I need to attend to. Your husband will know what to do."

He told himself he had done the job they hired him for, and that was enough. In the code he had worked out for himself, it was right to do what he had done and wrong to go beyond that. Justice of a sort might say Rick Mendoza deserved to be behind bars, but he had seen the way the guy handled himself on the mat.

Though he wouldn't make the call, he knew Judy Lathrop would make it, or insist her husband make it.

CHAPTER 38: THE HAWK'S CRY

THE NEXT MORNING, though she usually slept late after a night's patrol, Lucy paced outside the kitchen, the pup close behind her. Above the creek, at the top of a cypress, a crow called out insistently. Inside the weaving studio, as the four women sat down at the looms, the crow's call sounded above the hum of the heater.

Caw. Caw. Caw.

Her cell phone vibrated against Claire's hip. She pulled it out.

"Well, thank goodness you're answering," Judy said. "Mom, they've found Rick Mendoza. He's in the Schoonerville area near where you are, Mom. At some estate."

"Yes, I know."

"What do you mean you *know*, Mom? The local police are on their way now. Be careful, Mom. He's violent. I'm so upset by all this that I've canceled my appointments for the day. I'm in the park, taking a walk near the Jerry Garcia amphitheater. I hope they find him soon. Are you all right?"

"Yes, we're about start weaving here," Claire said.

"You're getting ready to *weave*, Mom?"

In the stream beneath the weaving studio, Rick checked gabions. Four firm rows on the upstream side of the Bridge now steadied the bank and one end of the weaving workshop. He walked downstream, out of the shadow of the studio. Yesterday's digging had left an abrupt opening in the bank. It was not a good place for a hole, but they'd finish on that side today.

Something stirred, a restlessness in the air and in the rocks of the streambed that reminded Rick of tensions he had felt in the Afghan hillside before the next explosion. A crow dropped from the top of a cypress tree and flew toward him, nearly swiping his face before swerving toward the weaving studio. Ashford ran out the door, trembling, staring at Rick.

I struggled to communicate with Rick, to tell him what I suddenly knew. What Ashford and the trees and rocks knew. *Move, Rick. Now. Get them out.* But he hesitated, puzzled and unaware.

The Animals had insisted that I must not Enter human beings, and I feared the old seductive greed for a human body. But my fear collapsed before my need to communicate with Rick.

And so I entered him. My substance filled his body,

237

the heavy gift of human flesh joining with whatever presence was mine. And, in that moment before the earth began to shudder, Rick understood what we had to do.

We—I—how do you say it—scrambled up gabions to the top of the stream bank, Rick's right leg aching from the exertion. We hurled ourselves into the weaving studio where Maria was poised to send the shuttle across the open warp, and Claire's left hand gathered up warp threads. Jean and May were sorting wool.

"Get out of here! Get out! Now!"

The urgency of the shout startled the women from their work and sent them running toward the door. Maria and May reached safety first. Claire and Jean were still inside when the earth shrugged for the first time and the weaving studio's grip on the stream bank loosened. As the building began to slide, Rick and I helped Jean over the threshold of the studio to Maria and May. Claire, farther back in the studio, was thrown to the ground as looms toppled around her. As the ground heaved again and the studio slipped from its moorings, we ran toward where she lay under a fallen loom. We pushed it aside and picked her up, limp in our arms.

By now the workshop had slipped farther into the creek, and the top of the embankment where the others stood was well above our heads. "Lift her! Lift her up!" Jean cried, stretching her body over the edge of the embankment, her arms reaching down toward where we held Claire, while behind her May held Jean tightly by the hips. But, as the weaving studio sank farther onto the stream bed, the gap between us widened.

Far above I heard the high keening that had released me from the Stuckness. Claire stirred, her eyes opened and she lifted her arms towards Jean.

But the gap remained. The extra strength I'd counted on when I entered Rick wasn't there. What had made me think he and I could truly join? I'd tried to understand what he'd gone through, had cheered for his efforts to change, had faced my jealousy about our blood connection. But it hadn't been enough.

And now the gap, too big to breach, widened.

We strained into the space, came half an inch closer, an inch. Not enough. Again. Not. Enough. We yearned upward, lifting her, reaching beyond hope of any ordinary kind.

Above us, on the bank of the stream, Dog appeared. He stood motionless, ears erect, eyes sparking. Wings, raven-black and mallard-motley, surged powerfully into the space that separated Claire from the others. Claire's hands, both the warm one of flesh and the silver one, reached beyond possibility and touched Jean's hands. And she was lifted to safety.

Time fractured again, and Rick and I fell back into darkness as the beams of the studio collapsed.

After Greg went to work, Judy left their house and, full of worrying energy, headed up Silver Avenue to check on our place. Nothing was amiss there, so she walked up the wooded Peru Street stairs to McLaren

Park, past the water tower and down the slope lined with acacias already hinting of gold, toward the reservoir with its circle of dark stones thrust up from the Pacific tectonic plate. She spoke with Claire, then waited for her cell phone to ring with the news that Rick was in custody. Mallards swam in the pond as always, making V's across the water — two males with iridescent heads and striking plumage and a female in delicate shades of brown. Out on a cypress branch, a crow muttered to himself.

Judy walked briskly around the reservoir, past dogs swimming to retrieve balls tossed into the water, to the peninsula that curved into the reservoir, where the resident egret stood on a thin black leg gazing hopefully into the water. Judy sat down on a flat-topped boulder, took out her cell phone and checked her messages.

The earthquake arrived in San Francisco a few seconds after it hit Piper Creek; shuddering into McLaren Park in a terror of shrieking trees, crashing trunks and branches. Judy crouched down beside the boulder, as the waves of shock unrolled and the roots of a nearby cypress gave up their grip. The tree sighed soundlessly in the uproar and fell toward her.

Rick and I were trapped on the floor of the studio, which lay tilted against the stream bank. Water poured in through the shattered windows and rose around us. He was unconscious, barely breathing. I was awake, feeling the places in him where things hurt badly.

As I waited inside the body of the man who'd been

240

responsible for my death, I felt sad that his efforts were ending this way. Because of him, Claire was safe. And he wouldn't be here, trapped, finished, if he hadn't made himself available. If he hadn't been here on the Estate.

The edge of something caught my eye, a pattern of curving black and brown lines I couldn't identify, the way you see the mysterious edge of a book cover peeking out between other volumes. My eye traveled into the design, and I realized that Dog's paw and foreleg, Raven's wing tip and Mallard's prodding beak were poking into the substance I shared with Rick. With their help, I found my way out. I didn't want to leave him, but Raven signaled that I should let things take their course.

"I'm sorry," I told them. "I see now that whatever I tried with Rick wasn't enough. Sometimes I still resented him."

"*Quawwkkk,*" said Raven. "Don't you know that it can never be enough?"

It was a humbling thought, in tune with other thoughts. It was obvious that I hadn't observed the Animals' restriction about entering human bodies, and I mentioned that. "It was what I felt I had to do, but even so it wasn't enough to fill the gap."

They let me know there is a Higher Obedience, and I had chosen it. That Gaps are needed, vivid with longing, and the usual sort of perfection is not what fills them.

Above us on the embankment, May was calling to someone, "Rick's still down there."

241

"They'll come for him now," Mallard said. And Dog gave me a look that said it was time to head south.

We arrived in McLaren Park as the shaking stopped and silence fell over the reservoir. Judy lay unconscious in the angle of the fallen cypress, its jagged bare branches reaching out around her like prickly guardians. A yellow butterfly ventured past and alighted on the fallen tree. A spider crawled along the bark of the cypress and onto her outstretched hand. The egret flew back to his fishing place.

She was breathing.

I watched as Mallard's elegant wings, the glossy shine of Raven's feathers, Dog's sleek nose disappeared into the slipstream of her subconscious. I could see the forms that lighted up within her--my face, her mother's, a schoolyard garden, her first teacher, a battered child, the tree outside our window at home--strands of a net that vibrated across time. And there came other images, Greg's face, full of his steady kindness . . . and a baby reaching out her arms.

Judy woke to see a young man standing over her, attached by leashes to three scrambling, yapping small dogs. "We'll get you out in a minute, ma'am," he said. "You've been pinned by one of the branches. It looks like the trunk just missed you." Later, the doctor at a first-aid station put her broken arm in a sling. Greg was with her by then.

Back at the creek, the gabion crew ran toward the fallen studio, smashed out the picture window and climbed in. A loom had fallen across Rick, its half-

242

finished weaving draped around his body. Dave knelt beside him and announced that he was breathing. Taking a loom with an intact weaving, the men improvised a stretcher on which they laid Rick, passed it through the window and carried it downstream to a place where they could climb up the bank and return to where the women ministered to Claire, and where, in a little while, Rick opened his eyes.

During the long wait on the bank, the women made Claire and Rick as comfortable as they could. Someone will surely come soon, they told themselves, listening to the stream trickle past the studio that lay partly submerged below them. Finally, they heard a vehicle in low gear, crawling around fallen trees, and the old man and Garth arrived in the estate's pick-up truck. Seeing the half-drowned studio, they turned in wonder and concern to the little group of women tending to Claire and Rick.

Jean told how Rick had appeared to warn and rescue them from the studio as it collapsed in the earthquake. "If he hadn't gotten us out, we'd still be down there," she said. "I don't know how he did it."

The old man said to Rick, "We know who you are, no use hiding it now." The light of recognition shone on Rick then, and he let it be there.

They skirted fallen trees on a circuitous route back to the center of the estate, where the main house and the outbuildings had mostly held together, with minor damage. What had been overturned could be set right. Lucy and Ashford became acquainted and went on

243

separate investigations of the scene. The puppy crept out from under a shed and headed for Lucy.

"Your mom's all right," Greg said to Judy. He'd called north to the police at Schoonerville, who told him that the women in the weaving studio had escaped just before the studio jackknifed into the stream.

"And they've found Rick Mendoza. He got the women out of the workshop just before it collapsed. He rescued your mom and the other women. He'd been on the estate for a while, going by another name. Nothing's really sorted out yet. He got them out, then was trapped and injured when the shed collapsed."

"The trial can go ahead, once he's well enough," Greg added. "They'll have to pick a jury, which takes a while. Meantime he's in the hospital."

Judy nodded, letting the news soak in. Sorting things out.

CHAPTER 39: WHERE WE ARE NOW

CLAIRE, scheduled to be the major witness in an open and shut case of vehicular manslaughter, made an appointment with the prosecuting attorney. "Rick Mendoza saved my life," she said. "I won't testify against him. He's working at rehabilitating himself. You can talk to Mr. Walter Adams about him, too, and other people he worked with on the estate. I'm satisfied and I'm sure my husband would be satisfied, too. I'm withdrawing myself as a witness."

The prosecuting attorney, a man who liked to make clear that he had the power of the law to uphold, told her she could be required to testify or face penalties. But since the chief witness in the case was unwilling to testify for reasons of conscience, the case collapsed and Rick was freed.

The support group caught up with Claire. "Honey,

thank the Lord you're back where phone calls get through," Francie said. Claire talked to Edith and Don, and, amazingly, to Jeff. "Hello," he said in his formal way. "I'm glad you made it back okay." He receded into warm silence.

Houses like ours in the Excelsior, which had not been on the main fault line, weren't much damaged in the quake. In McLaren Park, a few of the rocks fringing the reservoir had loosened and tumbled into the water. Elderly trees, like the one which pinned Judy to the boulder, were down. Still, the quake was not the Big One—not for us, not this time.

When she met again with the support group, Claire asked if Rick could be invited to the group. Don said he'd like to have someone in the group with similar issues and experiences. Jeff, who didn't disappear into his room as often these days, looked interested, too. Edith and Francie nodded their agreement and spoke of "working to get free of things" and "dealing with losses." And so Rick became part of the support group. He and Don met with the others, and for a time with each other, in silence or conversation, letting the parade of horrors, of twisted honor and duty, of loyalty and betrayal, pass before them as they spoke of memories which slowly lost their hold.

The vastness of cyberspace could hardly hold all the earthquake stories; one story, no matter how sensational, couldn't take up too much room. The residents of Schoonerville held the line, looking much put upon by the end of the week at roving paparazzi shoving TV cameras in their faces. The Adams estate remained politely but firmly closed to visitors. The case of a fugitive veteran soon evaporated from the media.

The rugs in the weaving studio were a mess, drenched with mud and water, torn as the looms careened around the studio. There'd be a work of salvage, of building new looms and weaving new rugs with the ancient images of mountains and trees and animals. The studio itself was beyond repair, and Dave Jackson began sketching a new Bridge undergirded with supports which he and Garth and the others would test for flexibility and strength.

When I checked in on Maria's dreams, the dream-space had a good feel to it. I stashed a new prop in a corner where I hoped she'd find it--a portrait I've painted of Rick, clear-eyed and kind, as he's becoming. He'll be at the Estate soon, still carrying her image in his own dreams. At that moment, the door opened in Maria's dream, and the dreamer herself came into the room. She saw Rick's portrait, ran to it and picked it up, laughing and surprised by her own joy.

When Claire meets you, it's with a friendly touch of her left hand, and a greeting, even a handshake, from the silver hand. The insurance company might eventually come up with enough money for one of those bionic hands, if she decides she wants one. She continues to weave, sometimes at home, sometimes at the estate with May and Maria and Jean.

I watch beside her at night and like to stand at the edge of her dreams, looking in. The other night she

247

appeared dressed in green and white, spring itself. Dog showed up, carrying in his mouth the dragonfly notebook I've been writing in. "Read it to her," he said. "Tell her your story."

It was an offer of communication that went beyond my wildest desires for contact. I recoiled, the remnants of the tatters flapping. "I can't put her in danger again," I told him.

"It might not be quite like that, dear," Mallard said.

"*Quawwwkk*. Such restraint."

Dog waited, and the notebook transformed itself into a magnificent long-stemmed rose. He let me know that if I gave Claire the rose this could be a good thing. So I walked into Claire's dream, rose in hand, and carefully held it out to her. And with equal care she took it in the silver hand and rested the petals against her cheek. Our eyes met, and we joined each other outside of fear and time, inside the flower's gift of silence.

The line of our blood is in a new being growing inside Judy, a granddaughter who will be Claire's delight and mine. In the meantime, Candace and I still spend quality time together. When she's born, I hope to watch her as she turns into the dancer I know she'll be.

I'm sitting with Candace at one of the tables in the circular restaurant just off the golf course. She's having a spritzy drink and I'm nibbling some good gruyere. On the far side of the room, W.C. Fields is at a table, penciling something on a notepad, maybe one of those inventions he works on with Hedy Lamarr. Occasionally, he glances in our direction, then goes back to his drink and the notepad. "He's waiting for Elena," Candace says.

At a table halfway around the room, a man with gray, wistful eyes gazes in my direction.

"Candace," I say to her, "there's someone you've got to meet." I take her hand and walk toward my father, bowing inside all the way. Belting it out:

"Shave and a haircut . . . two bits!" And then we're all hugging each other and sitting down together at his table.

The year is almost up since the accident, and the Animals remind me that the Thread connecting me and Claire and Rick will disappear on the anniversary of my death.

I ache on hearing that, and Raven eyes me. "Lose that ye may find," he croaks.

I do understand something about that. I don't know what I'll find when the connection with Claire goes away. But today the light here is bright, and the View stretches a long way. Its Gaze touches everything that's spun and measured and woven, all the linking Threads that forever appear and disappear.

While I can, I tag along with Claire and Ashford on their morning walk up to McLaren Park and its blue tower. This morning you could see all the way from the bay to the ocean along the Alemany Gap, a flyway for seabirds between the southern hills of the city. The gulls had a tail wind as they headed in full sun toward the sea; later, as winds and tides changed, they'd fly back to feed in the bay.

High above us, a hawk lifted in an expanding spiral, and I thought of Hawkling and our flight together. By now he must be full grown, a soaring presence watching over the Estate. Something tugged hard at me then as I watched the hawk set a course toward the Gate.

Thanks for reading *The First Year of My Death*. For more information about Mary Stein and her books, please go to <ins>Marysteinbooks.com</ins>

.

www.ingramcontent.com/pod-product-compliance
Lightning Source LLC
Chambersburg PA
CBHW031316040426
42443CB00005B/92